Born, raised and now living in rural Lincolnshire, Elisabeth is a proud mum to three boys, two dogs and a cat (that replaced her now ex-husband). When not struggling to keep three small humans alive, Elisabeth can be found teaching 'Outdoor Education' around schools in the county, being overly competitive and drinking gin with her mates.

To my three gorgeous boys: it is an absolute pleasure to be your mummy. Thank you for all the great material for this book. Keep it coming for book number two.

To my wonderful family and to Emma and Rupert who became part of that family. I honestly don't know where I would be without you.

Elisabeth Mary

3 BOYS, 2 DOGS, 1 (EX) HUSBAND AND ABSOLUTELY NO IDEA

Definitely not a guide to parenting (or marriage)

AUSTIN MACAULEY PUBLISHERS™

LONDON · CAMBRIDGE · NEW YORK · SHARJAH

A CIP catalogue record for this title is available from the British Library.

ISBN 9781398423428 (Paperback)
ISBN 9781398423435 (ePub e-book)

www.austinmacauley.com

First Published 2022
Austin Macauley Publishers Ltd®
1 Canada Square
Canary Wharf
London
E14 5AA

I never realized how many people it took to publish a book. Thank you to each and every one of you for your hard work and your patience.

Hannah, thank you for making me write my thoughts down on paper and for laughing and crying when you read them. Without you there wouldn't be a book.

Definitely not a guide to parenthood but a must read for those who feel they're doing a terrible job (you can't be any worse than me!).

Foreword/Spoiler

I never really meant to write a book. This all started because my sister enjoyed my ridiculous 'WhatsApp' messages about life. When, with her encouragement I decided to put it all together and write a book, my intention was to talk about the bits of pregnancy and parenthood that aren't so often talked about, make people feel a little less alone, a little less like a failure (how I spend most of my time) and of course to make people laugh.

It has taken a lot longer than I ever thought it would to get it written. It's taken a back seat to music groups, sports clubs and to 'me time' in the evening. That hour when you've put the children to bed, tidied the house and sit down to watch something utterly pointless on TV. That hour you totally regret the next morning knowing you should have gone to bed because now you're utterly exhausted and all you can think about is climbing into bed again that night (even though you already know you won't because you will be desperate for that hour of 'me time').

Anyway, I digress. The book has taken me a lot longer than I thought to write. In that time my life has taken an unexpected turn. I find myself in a position I never imagined, as a single mum to three boys and two dogs with one husband that no longer wants to be married to me. My husband decided he wanted to separate 15,000 words in. It has been very difficult not to go back and edit those 15,000 words to make him look like a total bastard. I'm glad I haven't because it wouldn't be true (not totally anyway) and if nothing else this book is truthful. However, along the way I have reflected on events or relationships from where I am now, so bear with me. This really is a truthful depiction of life since I peed on that stick.

I hope you enjoy it so much that you clamor for a sequel. Perhaps it could chart my rise from rock bottom where this book leaves me, to finding happiness again! Let's hope!

Varicose Veins...In My Vagina?

I hated being pregnant! There, I've said it. Cue gasps of shock and pregnant women everywhere cradling their bumps. Let me clarify, I didn't hate my unborn child. However, for what is essentially ten months I hated my life!

It wasn't even the tiredness, nor the incessant need to wee twelve times a night. It wasn't my husband waking me up just after I'd fallen asleep (after hours of maneuvering my ginormous whale like body into a comfortable position) because "you're sleeping on your back and I've read in my 'expectant dad book' that it's not good for the baby". Yes, that's horrendous but you are so grateful when it's gone that a newborn waking every three hours/hour/twenty-five minutes seems like luxury!

It wasn't my growing tummy that made me want to fast forward the miracle that is pregnancy. No, I enjoyed being able to eat what I wanted because of my 'cravings': Chips with pregnancy number one (only from the chippy and most definitely not oven chips); marmite and tomatoes on white toast with lashings of butter with number two and Cadbury's Crème Eggs with number three (he arrived shortly after Easter).

My growing bump allowed me to indulge in a new wardrobe. "No love, it's not maternity but it's stretchy so I can wear it after too," was a favorite saying of mine. Then of course you realise that you are the size of a baby elephant, and not only do you need maternity clothes, but you need them two dress sizes bigger than you would normally wear! Before you know it, you've wasted hundreds of pounds in Top Shop and you're still wearing the revolting maternity clothes you thought you would need for a couple of months when your youngest is two!

No, what really did it for me in pregnancy was the varicose veins in my vagina! With Baby Number One these arrived over night at about twenty-two weeks. I went to bed with a normal noo, noo. By morning it had turned into a swollen monster which made me feel like I was sitting on a tire. Of course, cue mad panic; cue making my poor husband look; cue making my poor husband hold a mirror so I could look; cue phoning the doctors' surgery in tears. "What do you mean the doctor can't see me until 3:25 pm? Tell him my vagina is falling out!" Anyway, apparently, it's quite common and true to the doctor's words it disappeared straight after the birth. Can't say the same for the varicose veins on my legs, but that's another story! Although prepared for this to occur with baby number two and three, I didn't think it would happen before I'd even peed on a stick!

I have to say that apart from this my pregnancies (from my point of view anyway) were medically speaking quite a smooth run. With one exception. Let me set the scene: I'm thirty-eight weeks pregnant with Baby Number Two, Baby Number One is twenty months old. I'm homeless. This is not quite as dramatic as you may first think, we'd sold our first home and hadn't yet quite managed to buy our second, so I was living with my mum and dad whilst my husband stayed with friends in London to avoid the commute (and his heavily pregnant wife!) Anyway, I was homeless and being waited on hand and foot by selfless parents. I got a headache late afternoon, took a paracetamol, chastised myself for not drinking enough, etc. I made it through bath time and settled down to read Baby Number One his favorite bedtime story which at that time was Julia Donaldson's, 'The Scarecrow's Wedding'. I kept fumbling words and just couldn't get them out. I went to bed and woke a few hours later with a blinding headache but more worryingly I felt that my fingers were swollen (they weren't). Downstairs to find my mummy, the oracle of all baby related questions. "Phone the midwife," she says, so of course I phone the midwife.

After a somewhat garbled conversation in which I made little or no sense I was asked to come into the maternity unit immediately. Daddy to the rescue! Somewhat reluctantly he stops his piano practice, removes his slippers, and starts the car. We arrive at the hospital. "This is Elisabeth," he announces at reception as I was now unable to speak. "And I am the father, but not of the baby, the mother, it would be illegal to be both!" I saw the receptionist press the button for social services there and then.

The next few hours should have been scary, but I felt so ill and so embarrassed as my father in his vicar uniform attempted to chat up the nurses that I didn't really comprehend the severity of the situation, they were concerned that I may have had a stroke. Dad clearly didn't pick up on this either because once he'd flirted up a storm he asked, "Are you going to keep her here? Because if you are,

I'll go home. I've got an early service tomorrow." It wasn't even a Sunday!

Anyway, turns out it was just a migraine and once I could say, 'baby hippopotamus' they sent me home. Well, Dad came to collect me and was only one hour and forty-five minutes late!

I think I was lulled into a false sense of security with Baby Number One, it was a straightforward pregnancy and a straightforward birth. My husband and I enjoyed our twelve week and twenty-week scan. We worried for nothing except who was going to look after the dogs when we went into the hospital and of course whether the number of chips I'd eaten might affect our unborn child. Therefore, we went off to the twelve-week scan with Baby Number Two with a skip in our step. Within seconds of the scan beginning the sonographer turned off the machine and asked us to wait in the little room down the corridor where a specialist midwife would come and speak to us.

Well, I promptly started crying hysterically! Looking back, I must have terrified the poor people waiting to go in. Anyway, our baby had a nuchal translucency (that's the sack of fluid at the back of the neck measured at the twelve-week scan) of 6.4mm. If this measurement is over 2.3mm it is an indicator that a baby may have a chromosomal abnormality or a congenital defect.

Unfortunately, the specialist midwife was unavailable, and we weren't perhaps given all the information. At no point were we told that actually your baby could be totally fine, it's just an indicator and to this day my husband and I are adamant she used the words 'not a viable pregnancy'.

The next forty-eight hours are a bit of a blur. My mum who was babysitting for us tells me our conversations were comparable to a conversation with a dolphin: High pitched and non-sensical. During those forty-eight hours I had a phone call from Birmingham Women's Fetal Medicine Department. That title today fills my heart with joy but at the time I could only feel dread. My husband and I went there at the end of forty-eight hours. We met the Professor (when I picture him, I always think of a character similar to Dr McDreamy from 'Grey's Anatomy'. It really shocked me when I googled him whilst writing this book to find that he does not look like him at all, quite the opposite in fact), he performed a CVS a chronic villus sample. This is similar to an amnio synthesis, but a sample is taken from the placenta and not from the amniotic chord.

He told the quivering wrecks that were my husband and I that baby looked great and that there was more likely nothing wrong than something wrong...WHAT? I had put us on the prayer list of every church I knew, signed myself off work for the foreseeable future and cried more than I'd ever cried before and here he was telling me what I thought I'd never here. Obviously, I cried some more but these were happy, relieved tears now.

You may have noticed a recurring theme here? I cry...A lot! Happy? I cry! Sad? I cry! Angry? I cry! Tired? I cry! Pretty much any emotion? I cry!

The initial test results took seventy-two hours. These ruled out any chromosomal abnormalities. I couldn't take that phone call, the husband had to take it at work. It came back all clear. He cried. I cried some more. A sixteen-week scan showed baby's heart and other major organs showed no sign of abnormality and that we were expecting baby boy number two. I cried some more. Then we had a twenty-week scan, baby all healthy! I cried some more. Then we had a 24, 28, 32, 36 and 38-week scan, baby all healthy. I cried some more (every time).

I'm not going to lie, perhaps another reason that I hated pregnancy withstanding the varicose veins was worrying all day every day. Has baby moved? Is that my waters trickling or have I weed myself? Will my obsession with programs about serial killers and prisons affect my fetus? Why can't I feel my pelvic floor muscles? Can I afford a designer vagina?

Unfortunately, this worry didn't stop with the birth of any of my children. Now I just worry about different things instead. Did I pay the middle one enough attention today or is he going to develop a complex? I forgot to brush my nine-month-old's teeth will they fall out? I have my smear test, will they be able to find my cervix? Does my husband mind that he has to sleep in the spare room every night, or more worryingly does he prefer it? The list is endless...

Whilst pregnant with number two my husband and I agreed that we couldn't do this again. We were worried that my body didn't carry enough water to allow for the tears and we were happy with our two boys. But...A bit like the pain of childbirth you forget, well at least until you are in it again. So, on a beautiful family holiday nine months after giving birth to a healthy (albeit ginger) boy, Baby Number Three was joyfully conceived. Joyful for the obvious reasons but also because my husband and I had managed at least fifteen (okay maybe ten) minutes alone!

I dreaded the twelve-week scan and I was right to do so. My husband spotted the nuchal translucency straight away. I think the sonographer was slightly shocked when he asked her for the measurement. She was also probably slightly relieved as she didn't have to have the conversation with us. The sack measured 5.4mm. Here we go again I thought!

I didn't know this until afterwards, but my husband found the second time around a lot more difficult that the first. He didn't show it. He was a tower of strength immediately getting us referred back to Birmingham and back to my knight in shining armor. He refused to discuss the what ifs and because of him I remained cautiously optimistic. Obviously, I cried, but a little less than the time before. Baby three was born as healthy as they come (despite consuming his own meconium) after all the same tests and all the same scans. It just goes to show that modern medicine is an amazing thing but that an indicator is just an indicator, it is not a diagnosis.

Whilst we underwent the rigorous testing with baby number three, I remember watching a fantastic documentary on the BBC, 'A World without Down's Syndrome?' Comedienne Sally Phillips, the proud mother of a child with downs syndrome allowed us into her and her family's life, she questioned the ethics of pregnancy screening and explored the proposed new screening test. I remember saying to my husband, "I don't care anymore…I think I'm a good enough mum to cope with whatever condition our baby may have." I hope I meant that statement, that the strength and love and happiness I saw in that documentary would have been something I could have carried through into my own life. When we knew there might be something 'wrong' with our baby we never discussed not undergoing the tests even though they came with a one percent chance of miscarriage. At the time one percent didn't seem a risk, but I have looked back at that decision and thought what if we were that one in 100? We wanted all the information available to inform a decision that we were lucky enough never have to make. I look back at this time often. What would I have done? Would we have been able to make a decision? Would we have agreed? Would one or both of us have to live with regret forever?

When we had finished with the tests and the scans, we briefly discussed the 'what ifs'. Safe in the knowledge that our baby had no detectable underlying conditions. My husband shocked me because he would have terminated that pregnancy for reasons that I would not. I'm not saying he was wrong and I was right. Everyone has their reasons. We never discussed it again and looking back maybe that's why we never discussed it before because we knew that the lines, we had drawn in our own minds were miles away from each other.

Now, as a single mum of three boys the likelihood of ever being in that position seems highly unlikely. I cannot imagine anyone wanting to see me naked ever again! However, I would like to think if I was ever lucky enough to be pregnant again? I would do it my way!

False Starts

With Baby Number One I had no idea I was in labor. Looking back I missed some obvious signs: Contractions, the need to go for a poo all the time, my cervix dilating from a cheerio to a doughnut, but it is so drummed into you by every book and every ante-natal class that your first labor develops slowly, takes hours and that you shouldn't bother doing anything about it until you have 'four in ten' that when my contractions started extremely painfully and constantly my husband who was timing them on his app stated, "These can't be proper contractions, they're not coming regularly." So, I continued to dance around the kitchen whilst racing upstairs when the contractions gave me the need too for the next thirty-five minutes. My husband and the dogs enjoyed thirty-five minutes of Harry Potter, he was gutted when I told him we needed to go to the hospital (so were the dogs).

I'm not going to go into details about my labor, one of the things (yes another) that I hated in pregnancy was all the horrendous birth stories you hear. It's one of the reasons I only attended pregnancy yoga for two sessions...Halfway through the session we sat in a circle and heard the birth stories of the women who had previously attended the group.

Well, they were horrific! The other reason in case you are interested is that heavily pregnant women breathe really loudly and so it's not so relaxing when sandwiched between them. I have always had a thing about people breathing. When sharing a bedroom with my elderly grandmother whilst she recovered from toe surgery, I had to ask her to stop breathing whilst I fell asleep. She survived and I slept well.

What I will say about the birth of all three of my children is that I enjoyed them. Genuinely. Yes, it hurt! Yes, I pooed myself! Yes, I needed stitches! However, I was in control for the first time in my pregnancy and I relished it. Unlike my sister who whilst pushing out her first baby screamed at her husband. "My clitoris is falling off." Apparently, the doctor and midwife looked at her panic-stricken husband and reassured him. "Nope, it's still there." Another three babies have come out of her vagina since then and I think it's still intact, it's not really something we talk about.

Perhaps because labor number one took me by surprise, (I'm not sure how when he was four days late) I looked out for early signs of labor in my other pregnancies. I can't even count the number of times I sent my husband a photo with the caption, 'I think my mucus plug has fallen out'. He was very patient and never got too cross when I made him endure the two-hour commute to my parent's house because I thought I was having contractions…I wasn't.

At thirty-four weeks pregnant with Baby Number Two we went on holiday to Brittany. The second week was spent with my family, I am one of five children and at that time we had nine children between us. Yes, it was as dysfunctional but as fun as you imagine. We spent our days on empty beaches; wrapped in several layers I would sit my heavily pregnant self on a deck chair and watch Baby Number One eat sand whilst the men took part in beach cricket (they called them test matches but the only thing they tested was their wives' patience).

At the time Baby Number One had an obsession with snails. I spent the morning clambering over rocks with him prizing the unsuspecting snails from their homes, dropping them in a bucket where they would spend a few hours before we returned them to their natural habitat. By lunch time I was feeling a bit uncomfortable. I went for a little walk, no need to panic I thought. Then the pains became stronger and no matter what position I put myself in they wouldn't go away. I started to panic. What happens if you have a baby in France? Will they let me take him home? Do I know 'I want an epidural!' In French? Did French women also poo themselves in labor or was that going to be a nasty surprise? My husband is a planner, he also knew that this kind of paranoid behavior was inevitable and had therefore spend a valuable few minutes on google and knew exactly where the nearest maternity unit was.

Leaving Baby Number One collecting snails with his cousins we went off to the hospital. The car journey was tense, the pain was now constant and obviously I was crying. We arrived at the hospital and with a lot of pointing at my bulging tummy and my husband gesticulating wildly to things flying out of my vagina we got directed to the maternity unit. On route I found myself desperate for a poo, oh Lord I thought, baby is coming out. I fled to the toilet and a few minutes later came out slightly sheepishly. That's right, I had trapped wind! Ever so painful but not apparently a sign of labor.

When he did come Baby Number Two came really quickly and therefore when pregnant with baby number three, I developed a fear that he would come so quickly we wouldn't make it to the hospital. The fear was quite precise: I was scared that we would get stuck at the railway crossing in between our house and the hospital and I would give birth in the boot with everyone in the queue watching!

I made my mother move in with us from due date therefore reducing the time spent waiting for her to get over to our house before leaving for the hospital (that bloody train line got in the way again). The hospital bag was in the car plus a black out blind (so the people in the queue wouldn't be able to see). A week overdue I got my first contraction and that was it we went to the hospital. On arrival I realised I hadn't actually had another contraction on the twenty-five-minute journey but an examination revealed that I was indeed in the early stages of labor and because of my history of quick labors they wouldn't send me home. Great I thought, baby will be here soon. But no, cue the longest labor ever!

All births are different, when pregnant with Baby Number One I was obsessed with 'One Born Every Minute'. There was a lady on it who gave birth in a pool whilst listening to music with her partner, she didn't make a sound. "That will be me," I told my husband. That wasn't me! I gave birth doggy style whilst mooing like a cow and sweating profusely. I have friends who had candlelit water births, friends who had C-sections, friends who had episiotomy's, forceps and sat on a cushion for weeks after but we were all lucky enough to have beautiful babies to show for it and therefore the stories are technically all the same.

The Aftermath

I read a lot of pregnancy books, I had an app on my phone which compared my unborn baby to a fruit, I had a birthing plan (although I didn't go as far as one friend who had it typed and laminated), I went to pregnancy yoga (for two sessions) and NCT (for all six). We talked a lot about birth and labor, the NCT instructor carried out a pretend C-Section on a table in the village hall we met in. We watched a video about the wonders of breast feeding and how the baby will wriggle up from my tummy to find my nipple straight from birth. We were shown how to use cotton wool and water to clean our babies for the first few weeks after they were born, and we raced to see who could do the poppers on a Babygro up fastest (much to my husband's disappointment I didn't win). Excuse my language but, what a load of bollocks!

Baby Number One was born at 2:20 am, by 4:00 am they'd moved me onto the post-natal ward and my husband had been sent home. I spent the next few hours lying on my back (it felt so good) staring at my new baby in awe, wonder and to be perfectly honest, fear. When he stirred an hour or so later, I leapt from my bed and attempted my first nappy change. I took my cotton wool balls and distilled water from my new changing bag. I lay him on my new changing mat and opened up his nappy. Two minutes later I had a screaming baby with cotton wool stuck all over the black tar that covered his lower half. I persevered but the situation was going from bad to worse. A hand came around the curtain from the bay next door holding a packet of baby wipes. Baby wipes? Chemicals? What about my baby's sensitive skin? By the time my husband arrived for visiting I was a convert and Baby Number One had a clean bottom.

Unfortunately, this did not stop the crying. Right, I thought time to try this breast-feeding malarkey. I put baby nipple to nose, he didn't get it! I brushed his nose with my nipple, nothing. I was beginning to feel a little flustered now. Was everybody on the ward judging me? Did they think I was a terrible mother because I couldn't stop my newborn crying? Did my baby not like me? Was my nipple too big? I pressed the buzzer. The midwife arrived and I'm not going to lie, she was slightly terrifying. She grabbed baby, grabbed my boob, and shoved the two together. It worked, he latched on. What nobody had warned me about was the pains you get when baby latches on. The contractions that don't produce a baby. And of course, you can't even wriggle around to get comfortable for fear that baby will come off the nipple and the process will start all over again. But it's okay, you're in a hospital, there's bound to be drugs on offer. Good drugs to take away the pain. Two paracetamol? They did as much good as when the midwife suggests them in the early stages of labor!

Breastfeeding did not come naturally to me; it really was a two-person job and by that I don't mean me and the baby. I mean me, the baby, my husband/mum/midwife. I had 'love bites' all over my boobs where baby had missed my nipples (maybe they weren't too big after all). Coated in lanolin they were already cracked and bruised. I knew that to go home I had to crack breast feeding and yet I just couldn't do it!

All I wanted to do was go home. Hospital wards are not the place for someone who doesn't like the sound of other people breathing. People seem to forget that the curtains separating you are not soundproof. I could tell you all about the lady to the left of mess bowel movements. I could tell you how tired the lady opposite me was and how she begged the midwifes to take her baby for a few hours so she could sleep. They wouldn't and at one point she threatened to sue them! I could tell you that the grandparents of the baby to the right of me did not like the name the parents had chosen. I knew this because they discussed it in the aisle again forgetting that that curtain is not a soundproof barrier! Unfortunately, the parents heard too and were not impressed. We had moments of high drama like when one of the mums took her baby down to the café without telling the midwife, you could have heard a pin drop as we all listened in to her being told off whilst thinking, *thank God that's not me!* Whilst inwardly cheering; *she's clearly doing an even worse job than me!*

Whilst my nipples may have been sore, my vagina was in pieces! What I still find hilarious is that I had just pooed myself whilst two people watched and yet I felt embarrassed about the midwife checking my stitches. Thank God for those huge maternity pads you have to wear, without them I wouldn't have been able to sit down.

I don't think there was a euphoric high, I was too uncomfortable for that but there were obviously some amazing memories from the aftermath: My baby meeting his grandparents for the first time, watching my husband cuddle his son, my first shower. I kid you not, that first shower was one of the best things I have ever experienced. That is until I returned to my baby and my bed mate (provider of the baby wipes) said, "I hope you haven't used soap, baby won't be able to find their trail to your nipple now!" She was obviously an NCT graduate too!

What the Hell Do We Do Now?

Nothing and nobody prepare you for the moment you walk out of hospital with your newborn baby. I'd been wanting to get out of there since the moment he'd popped out of my vagina but as my husband remortgaged the house to pay for car parking all I wanted to do was return to the ward. I felt good listening to all those other new mums' struggle as much as I was (although I was aware of the lack of sound proofing and so only whispered about my struggles). I loved that the midwives would arrive as I pressed my buzzer (not that I ever did because I was so adamant, I would prove that I had taken to motherhood like a duck to water). As the automatic doors closed behind me, I genuinely thought, *bloody Hell, what have we done?*

I spent the twenty-five-minute journey home with my hand on baby number one's chest and my face in his face just in case he forgot to breathe. My husband drove no faster than 29 mph all the way home, this is actually incredibly dangerous on dual-carriage ways. He later told me that he had felt totally overwhelmed with the sense of responsibility, he's not the only one!

Obviously, the dogs were delighted to see me, they'd watched all seven Harry Potter films and were ready for something new to binge on. We'd read a lot of literature about introducing the dogs to a new baby (there is a surprising amount on the subject). We'd even played them the sound of a crying baby sporadically throughout the night and day to get them used to it. This, in case you were wondering did involve us setting an alarm, creeping downstairs and scaring them senseless! How, we thought, will they react to this new creature who would take up so much of our time? Well as it turned out, they couldn't care less. A quick sniff revealed that this swollen, odd smelling thing was not edible, carried no treats and offered no form of walk and therefore was of no interest to them.

Baby Number One was still asleep. Should we leave him? Should we have a cup of tea? What happens if he wakes, and we have a hot drink and we burn him? Should we put the television on? Move at all? Oh God! What happens when he wakes up? Obviously, he woke up as we stood in the kitchen staring at him and the world did not combust.

On night something my milk came in. I woke to Baby Number One crying. I sat up and started crying. My malleable soft breasts had transformed in lumpy, bumpy basketballs. Unfortunately, my nipples were so full of milk that baby could not latch on. He became increasingly frustrated, and I became increasingly upset.

Fortunately, my mum was staying with us for a few days. A mother of five there is not much she doesn't know about babies. Obviously, she's my mum so I think she's the best, but she imparts wisdom without being a know it all, she sorts you out without you feeling like a failure. I know how lucky I am to have this. If she were up for it then I'd rent her

31

out to new mothers for an absolute fortune and would have no need to write this book. Unfortunately, she has fourteen grandchildren already and my little brother hasn't even started reproducing yet! I know what you are all thinking...What the hell do they do at Christmas?

Back to my engorged breasts. My mum sent my husband downstairs to make a cup of tea. She held the baby whilst I stood in a steaming hot shower with milk pouring out of me. I then had to pump a little from each breast and at last when my nipple was free from milk he could latch on. Having dreaded him waking up for a feed (because my nipples hurt) I was desperate for him to wake up and feed (because my nipples hurt). For the next three weeks or so hot showers, hot flannels and the breast pump kept me and the baby in 'comfort'. Your boobs do self-regulate but my God it takes some time! On more than one occasion my husband and I would wake up absolutely drenched. "Is it wee?" he once asked me. "No, it's bloody not!" I replied. "I've done my pelvic floor every time my 'squeezy' app told me too!" That was after Baby Number One, thank God he never asked again because that app got deleted midway through pregnancy number two and even, I questioned the dampness after the birth of Baby Number Three.

As I sit here thinking about my boobs, I'm reminded of a photo that I sent to my mummy friends on our whats app group soon after having Baby Number Three. Having had mastitis (a condition which causes a woman's breast tissue to become painful and inflamed) with both Baby Number One and two I was totally paranoid about getting it again. I had very sore nipples and swollen boobs and having spent a morning on google I sent my husband to the supermarket to get a cabbage. So off he went with Baby Number One and Baby Number Two in tow. They returned home what felt like several hours later with every cabbage that that supermarket and the other three in town had to offer. My poor husband had absolutely no idea what sort of cabbage to look for and was so scared that asking me might tip me over the edge (those bloody hormones) that I had a white cabbage, a savoy cabbage, and a red cabbage to choose from. A red cabbage? What was I meant to do with that? Pickle it and lay the strips over my nipples? What I didn't realise until my mummy friends replied to a photo of my bra stuffed with cabbage leaves is that the cabbage doesn't actually do anything. Once the coolness has worn off there is no purpose to the cabbage leaf. It will not soothe, it will not prevent mastitis, no, and all it does is make you smell like sweaty cabbage.

When Baby Number One was about five days old my mum went home. She's an incredibly strong woman and despite my husband and I both clinging to her ankles she managed to make it to her getaway car. Then after two weeks paternity leave my husband also left (to go back to work I hasten to add). So, it was just Baby Number One, me and the two dogs.

Looking back, I wish I'd stayed in my pajamas all day, slept when he slept (although I am yet to meet anybody who can sleep whilst pushing a pram, driving a car or walking around whilst carrying said child in a baby sling), binged on Netflix and as one of my close friends did get a camel Pak water system so she didn't have to get up to get a drink. I did these things (not the camel Pak) but probably not enough. Perhaps part of me was afraid to stay in the house with Baby

Number One all day, perhaps I'd read too much on early development, perhaps I wanted to prove to myself and everybody else that I was smashing parenthood, but I sought out organised fun. I loved nothing more than going to a group to waft a scarf in my newborn babies face.

On one occasion I bundled Baby Number One into the car and set off for our local woods to walk the dogs. I power walked for an hour or so sweating profusely because of course once you have a baby strapped to your chest you can't take off any layers (see toilet story). I climbed back into the car exhausted, checked the time, not even seven am. I drove home and pulled up on the drive. The next thing I remember is lifting my head off the steering wheel, opening my eyes to meet the eyes of next doors builders watching me as they had their elevens. Mortified I pull down the mirror to check what state I am in and have the imprint of VW in my forehead. I think that is the longest nap Baby Number One ever had!

Perhaps I regret not binging on Netflix etc. because I didn't get the opportunity to do that after the births of baby numbers two and three. I was in hospital for six hours after Baby Number Two was born. By lunchtime that day we were a full-fledged family of four. Four days later we have photos of me on an adventure playground. When we brought Baby Number Three home twenty-four hours after birth (they were worried he'd swallowed meconium and he needed to be monitored) we were getting the older two ready for bed when Baby Number One started vomiting. He continued vomiting for 48 hours. I remember the midwife coming to visit, Baby Number One was lying on the sofa puking (fortunately) into a bowl. Baby Number Two was (literally) climbing the walls and Baby Number Three was being fed. She looked at me and asked, "Have you not got someone who could take him out for a few hours?" Wearily my husband, who had just returned from the park raised his hand. Some of the best moments in those early days was when I managed to get all three to nap at the same time!

Once my husband had returned to work, I relied heavily on organised fun. The groups I used to go to out of choice. I now went to as a matter of survival. Yes, I could have stayed at home all day, but I am a terrible parent at home. I'm always saying, 'just let Mummy finish this', 'in a minute' or 'just one more Peppa Pig' I always have something to do: Washing, putting washing away, catching up with the TV I missed the night before and then I am wracked with Mum guilt because I haven't given them enough attention that day. So, going to a group for an hour where they have loads of activities you could do at home, but which would take you an hour to set up and two hours to tidy away was an absolute result!

Mum guilt should be its own chapter because it is always there, gnawing away (it's not going to be however because I don't want to give it the time). A good friend of mine, who is an amazing Mum to three beautiful girls, who always appears to have her shit together, whose children are always clean and dressed on the school run once said to me, "I feel like I would have been an amazing mum to one, a good mum to two but now I'm an average mum to three." She is not an average mum, but her mum guilt tells her she is. I battle with that thought a lot. I battled with it when deciding to have (or to stop trying to not have) another baby. It wasn't so much that I wouldn't have enough love to go around, it was more

35

would I loved one more than the other? Then once they were here it was, have I paid each of them enough attention? I definitely sang more nursery rhymes with the other two. I didn't read them a story each at bedtime and now they won't be able to learn to read until they're twelve. It's sunny and they are not outside doing physical exercise. They've watched too much television and it's not even the educational sort. I shouldn't have told them to wait until I'd hung out the washing, now they will feel rejected and will never have a meaningful relationship in their adult life. Whilst writing this I realise how ludicrous all my 'guilt' is, but it doesn't stop me feeling it. Whilst I write this Baby Number One is sat next to me doing a dot to dot, Baby Number Two is watching me type whilst asking me why the screen isn't playing, and Baby Number Three is sleeping. How on earth can I be feeling guilty about that? Well, I am. I should be doing that dot to dot with number one, teaching him about prime numbers or something similar, I should be discussing technological advances with number two, and I should be watching number three sleep thinking how lucky I am.

Mum guilt can fuck off! I do the best I bloody can and somedays I am better at mothering than others. There are some days when by nine o'clock in the morning my three have created beautiful pieces of artwork which I've already hung on the fridge. We've been for a walk with the dogs on which we discussed all the wonderful nature around us. The children skipped along happily or sat contentedly in the push chair. At lunch time they've eaten nutritious meals with little mess whilst we discuss serious issues that do not include poo and wee and then they've asked to leave the table. We spend our afternoons in the grounds of a stately home before going home to a tidy house and pre prepared tea. They then have half an hour's educational television before a bath, seven stories and bed. (Okay, I admit it, I don't think I've ever had a day like that, but all of those things have happened on different days.) Then I have days where I can only 'wade' through the number of toys and dirty laundry on the floor. When I've fed the three of them cold toast (from the night before) for breakfast in front of a program that has 'bum' in the title just so I can sit in the kitchen, drink a cup of tea and watch something on my phone. I've had days where the dogs have not been walked and instead their only form of exercise is being harassed by the children. But what I tell myself on these days is, it's okay, they feel loved, they are happy and so far, they are not showing any signs of being a serial killer. However, there are also the days when I think *fuck it, I can't do this* and so I walk out and leave them 'Lord of the Flies' style for the day...JOKE! I pack up the car with the three children and two dogs and drive them over to my mum and dad's for the day! It's okay to feel like that but it doesn't feel okay. It took me a long time to admit to anyone that it wasn't always fun, fun, fun! That somedays I didn't really like my children and that I found them really annoying. The Mum guilt comes gnawing and I don't know about anyone else, but I make the concerted effort to be a better mummy for at least the next 24...12...Okay, six hours.

Husband/Mother-in-law/Random Stranger: Why are they screaming like that? What has happened?

Me: I wouldn't let them unwrap all my sanitary towels and stick them on every available surface.

Husband/Mother-in-law/Random Stranger:(SILENCE)

The best thing about looking after/having a cuddle/playing with a child that isn't yours is that when they start crying/screaming/biting/kicking you can just pass them back to their parents. I can still feel the pressure I felt when someone would pass me back my screaming baby and I knew the expectation was that I, as their mother would to be able to calm them if not immediately then pretty quickly. Looking back this was actually quite easy, the sticking of a milky nipple in their face tended to do the job 99.9% of the time.

I have also come to the conclusion that as a child gets older it becomes less and less socially acceptable for them to be having the screaming ab-dabs in public. I don't care what anyone says the moment your child starts kicking off in public is the moment everyone around you starts judging. I do it! Although I'm less judgey and more relieved that it is not mine doing the kicking off.

Our first outing with Baby Number One was to John Lewis' in Solihull when he was 6 days old. It wasn't the greatest success for a number of reasons:

1. My husband and I's inability to open up the base of the pram. It was the first time since purchasing it that we'd collapsed it and despite the fact that between us we have three degrees and a masters, we could not get the bloody thing open. In a final act of frustration my husband kicked it (fairly aggressively) and it opened.

2. Baby Number One's inability to lie flat in a pram without crying. This in turn meant us constantly stopping, picking him up, soothing him, having a discussion about how it was too dangerous to just walk about with him to put him back in the pram walk three meters and repeat the process.

3. My inability to breast feed without taking my entire top half off. This meant that I couldn't sit in 'The Place to Eat' have a decaf latte whilst chatting to my husband and feeding my newborn like I had always imagined. What it actually meant was that I sat in the baby room, topless with milk gushing everywhere whilst my husband looked uncomfortable, hissing, "I don't think men are supposed to be in here." With me hissing dramatically back at him, "If you leave me alone in here you will NEVER see your child again!"

We called it quits and went home via McDonalds Drive Thru whilst the baby slept happily in his car seat and shopped online evermore. The End.

Except that is not why I told you this story. The point of this story is that my husband and I were so worried about the baby crying in public that we didn't manage to accomplish anything, we bailed! I'd like to say that as we had more children, the boys got older and we became more confident in our roles as parents that we learnt to accept that children do cry, that no one is really judging us and that the screaming/kicking/biting/hair pulling is just the child's way of expressing themselves. This is not the case. I still regularly abandon my shopping trolley halfway down the frozen food section because one or two of the boys are expressing themselves, 'I don't want to go with you!', 'don't touch me, you're hurting me!' and I come to the conclusion that if I don't make a break for it now someone is going to report me for kidnapping and abusing child. Just recently I had to remove Baby Number Three from Sainsbury's because he was laying on the floor throwing tantrum (he hadn't been allowed a bottle of Diet Coke, surprising that isn't it? At the age of two!) I couldn't carry him, too many flailing limbs so I attempted a tight grip of his hand. When this failed and he nearly killed himself escaping my vice like grip and running into the path of an incoming car I took him by the wrist. At this point he refused to move his legs and became a dead weight being dragged by one arm to the car whilst screaming. "don't put me in your car!" The feeling when I managed to wrestle him into the car seat and strapped him in so he could no longer move was almost orgasmic!

There are other days when I ride it out. Perhaps I feel more confident in my parenting on these days or perhaps it's because my bribe has worked, I just don't know!

I used to see children sat in trolleys being fed around supermarkets and think I would never do that. Now, when I put everything through the check out its basically only the bleach that hasn't got a bite out of it and trust me if I didn't

40

think it would kill them, I'd have let them try it just to walk away with the essentials relatively stress free.

I used to hear parents bribe their children. "If you sit down in the trolley, you can eat all five Freddo's in the pack." And I used to think I would never do that. Why don't they use 'the language of choice' so beloved by all teacher training facilities? Two options to choose from, both the result that you want. I'll tell you why…Because they haven't got the bastard time to be giving choices and just need to get some shit done! Now, I am an accomplished negotiator. I carry treats with me at all times and there are few situations that I cannot bribe my way out of. Does this make me a terrible mother? Probably. Do my children have me wrapped around their little finger? Yes. Does this mean that they are going to turn into sadistic serial killers? Maybe, but it gets me through my day so needs must!

I used to hear parents give empty threats. "If you hit your brother again then there will be no television for a week!" We all know that the moment you get home the one-eyed babysitter is going on so you can have a cup of tea/shot of vodka through the eyeball in peace! I would never do that! Except I do…All the time! I think my most common empty threat is, 'if you do that again then we will go home', I probably say this at least fourteen times before we do go home (and that's because the place is closing). However, on very rare occasions I follow through. It is always because actually it's time to go or because I want to go but the boys do not need to know this. These rare moments are great because not only do I feel like an excellent mother, whose got her shit together, with firm boundaries and clear consequences (like it says in all those parenting books) but I

41

can also then use it as an empty threat for a good few weeks without them realising its an empty threat. Now that my friends are excellent in parenting!

I think my husband struggles with the boys being noisy in public more than I do. Not just the tantrums but the general rowdiness. He does a lot of shushing and bribing and empty threats himself at this point...So at least I know our parenting is consistent!

I feel like I should clarify (before anyone reports me) that there are times I try to understand my children's frustrations and their needs. I get down on my knees, make eye contact, talk in a soothing voice, use my listening ears, and then think, what the fuck are you doing? It turns out that you cannot reason with a one, two, three, four, five or six-year-old especially if it's about any of the following true tantrum stories:

- Incessant screaming from Baby Number Two. "I don't want to go! You can't make me go!" whilst hiding under his bed. We hadn't suggested going anywhere and had no plans to do so.
- Baby Number Three going ape shit because I had changed his pooey nappy and put it in the bin. The only thing that stopped the crying was me taking the nappy out of the bin and putting it back on him. Fortunately, I had the foresight to pull a (carefully placed) clean nappy out of the bin and he (at 18 months old) wasn't savvy enough to notice.
- Baby Number One didn't speak to me for days because I stopped him putting the toy thermometer

from the doctor's kit up Baby Number Two's arsehole.

- The trampoline being too bouncy.
- Ice-cream being too cold.
- I flushed away a poo before they'd said goodbye and then couldn't get it back.
- I wouldn't let them play with matches/sanitary towels/washing tablets.
- I wouldn't let them ride on the dogs back.
- I spoke to someone on the phone for thirty seconds.
- I wouldn't let them pick up dog poo on our walk (it wasn't even our dog's poo!)
- I couldn't stop the wind blowing/sun shining/rain falling.
- When their brother looks out of their window in the car.
- Wanting another sausage and me giving them another sausage.

Point proven?

In all seriousness I know that all children have tantrums. I understand that it is their way of communicating with me when they cannot express their thoughts and feelings. I know they might just be telling me they are tired, hungry, and uncomfortable. That they are frustrated because they cannot get what they want or it's not actually what they want when they get it. I have a vivid memory of an eight-year-old me who had asked my mum to French plait my hair. She did. I didn't like it. I can remember that feeling of frustration bubbling up and having a massive tantrum. I'm sure my mum wouldn't have minded that I didn't like it if I had just said it. I wouldn't say I'm delighted my children have tantrums, but I would rather they did than they didn't. I remember reading something once that your child has a tantrum because they know they are safe to express themselves. I'll hold on to that in the frozen food section next time.

They've All Got
Their Little Fetishes

Baby Number One had Daisy. Daisy was a golden retriever cuddly that he took to at about six months old. He would suck his thumb and stroke Daisy's ears whenever he was chilling out. Otherwise, he carried her around with one ear. Daisy went everywhere with us, and God forbid we tried to get him to sleep or eat without her. Keeping Daisy safe and making sure she came home with us became more important than looking after the baby. We lost her once. It was awful. We were on holiday in Wales, we got back to the house, and she was nowhere to be seen. My husband went to look for her, he was gone hours. He was probably in fear of his life if he came back empty handed. At this point Baby Number One hadn't realised that she was missing, but it was only a matter of time. That time came when we strapped him in his car seat without Daisy. Even the promise of ice cream could not stem the screaming. Just as we left the village, I caught sight of something familiar hanging on the sign telling us to 'Drive Carefully' or 'Gyrru'n Ofalus'. There she was, I have never been so pleased to see anything or anybody in my entire life. About three months later he didn't want Daisy anymore, I know exactly where she is mind and could find her in a heartbeat if he started kicking off!

Baby Number Two never had a comforter. He's always been quite a grown-up baby, very serious and desperate to be with his big brother, he didn't have time for such nonsense. What did develop at the age of two and a half though was an obsession with other people's clothes. He is yet to grow out of this. I will send him to pre-school dressed for the day with spare clothes in his backpack only to pick him up in an outfit I've never seen before and only one a three-year-old can put together. What transpired is that he was taking items of clothing he fancies from various bags. He wears shoes seven sizes too big for him that a cousin has 'given' him. Only last night (Wednesday) I had to prize the clothes he'd been wearing since Sunday off him (he had taken them off for baths but hidden them so I couldn't wash them). I had to promise to have them washed and dry for him to put on in the morning. Are they his clothes? I can hear you ask. No, of course they're bloody not. We'd been for a play date, and he'd been 'given' them to wear...They are never getting them back!

Now, if you think that is odd, just wait until you hear about Baby Number Three. He likes skin. Yes, you read that right. I do worry that he may turn into Jean Baptiste Grenouille from the film 'Perfume the Story of a Murderer' who uses the skin of women to make perfume that encapsulates their smell. Freaked out yet? You should be! To begin with I thought he'd grow out of it after breastfeeding when he'd stroke/gently pinch my neck and chest. Then he started putting his hand down my top and pinching when he got tired. I stopped that, so now instead he aims for my armpit or my neck. I wouldn't mind but then his hand smells like my armpit. He also likes to knead his feet into skin, normally my tummy (squishy I suppose). The worst is when he fiddles with your earlobe and then when you least expect it, he puts a finger in your ear. The only 'positive' is that he doesn't do it to everybody...Just me and his eldest brother who doesn't mind. When he tries to do it to Baby Number Two, he shouts. "Mummy, he's touching me again and I don't like it!" I've had to reconfigure car seats as a result of this and have been known to say to Baby Number One, "Let him fiddle with your ear and then when he's asleep you can have a treat!'

You're probably thinking that my children are odd. They are. But just to put things in context. One of their cousins has a comforter called 'Stinky Sheep' so named because he reeks of snot, saliva, and rancidness and yet no one dare wash him for fear of him no longer being a comforter. At least stealing other people's clothes or playing with their mummy's skin is slightly more hygienic!

I didn't choose them as my friends because we drink wine on play dates, but it certainly helps.

I think I should clarify what I mean by 'Mummy friends', don't get me wrong I still have friends that aren't mums, I still have friends that I get together with when I don't have my children with me, and I value their friendship so highly. I had a friend say to me recently, "I love the fact that you are married, with three children and yet you still have your own life and do things for yourself." I didn't want to put her off by telling her that this night away (for a hen

47

do) had taken weeks' worth of preparation, organization, Mum guilt and angst and that I was not updating social media every five minutes (as they had falsely presumed) but messaging my husband for photo updates and news about poo etc.

As you will know from previous writing my husband and I are NCT graduates. The purpose of joining was so that I had people to eat cake and drink tea with. They could have been aliens, serial killers or laborites and I would still have been desperate to be friends with them. There were six couples in my NCT group and for the first six months of our babies lives the six mummies messaged incessantly, met up weekly and I had decided that they would all be God parents to Baby Number Two (they're not). There was nothing those ladies didn't know about my battered vagina, my gnawed nipples and my lack of sleep. However, as babies became older, and milestones began to be reached we (and I'm using the royal 'we' here because I presume, they felt the same) began to realise that actually apart from having babies of similar ages we didn't really have anything else in common. I for one began putting a glossy sheen on parenting because it had begun to feel a little competitive…"Flossie can now hold her fruit pouch by herself, whilst playing Mozart with her toes." The group began to split into smaller groups, smaller meet ups began to happen and by the time the babies were one regular contact ceased. I am still good friends with one of the five, she is actually Godmother to Baby Number Three. I follow the other four on social media and genuinely 'like' the photos and updates that are posted. They made the first moments of parenthood so much easier and enjoyable and for that I will be eternally grateful for our friendship.

We moved when pregnant with Baby Number Two, lived with my parents for six months and really the only people Baby Number One and I socialized with were family. Spending time with family is brilliant. I am proud that my family and I are all so close, some find it odd that we choose to socialize together and holiday together but it's just so easy! The cousins all play together, and it doesn't matter if they maim each other because they are cousins. There's no judgement about your parenting because they're your brothers and sisters and you wouldn't care even if they did judge.

Now, please don't get me wrong, we are no 'Brady Bunch' and certainly not the 'Von-Trapps'. Pretty much every time we're all together there is some kind of fall out. Fortunately, we all seem to be mellowing in our old age. Gone are the days of my middle brother calling the police because he thought my eldest brother was going to kill him. (My parents were slightly perturbed when the police responded with blue flashing lights and sirens.) Gone are the days of me flushing my sister's clothes down the toilet because she wouldn't let me borrow them. And gone are the days of my sister and I running across the front lawn screaming whilst the boys shot at us with their air rifles (the trick is to weave at speed!) These days our arguments tend to be passive aggressive and forgotten by the time we get all the children to bed.

For me, the thing about spending time with family is that you don't have to try, they love you and your children despite of and probably because of all your flaws. They know that when you lose it with your children it's because you're tired and you've tried cajoling, bribing and every other trick in your parenting bag before finally losing the plot. When they turn up you don't worry that the house is a mess, you've got no healthy snacks and you haven't brushed your teeth yet because now they're here you can probably rectify some of those things. You can tell them when you haven't got enough money to go to the soft play, when you've argued with your partner, when you think you have a lump in your boob or when your child has been in trouble at preschool for putting things down the toilet knowing that they want to know, will forget when they've left and probably won't think about it again. The best thing about spending time with family for me? You don't spend the twenty-four hours after they leave thinking through all the things you said, analyzing them and worrying that the person thinks you are a dick.

So, when we moved into our new home twenty minutes from my mum and dad I went on the hunt for 'Mummy friends' with whom I could feel like I did with family but that I was able to slag my family off too.

I am pleased to be able to report that I was successful in this mission. However, whilst in search of suitable candidates I spent a lot of time feeling quite lonely, turning up at toddler groups and spending the 90 minutes on the periphery of conversations whilst following Baby Number One ensuring he wasn't biting/pushing/hitting/climbing/running whilst feeding Baby Number Two. I spent many an hour on the phone to my husband who patiently listened and told me to keep trying and try I did. I smiled, asked people how old their children were, exclaimed at any similarities we might have. I proposed play dates to people I barely knew. I'd pain strikingly get the house ready to cancel at the last minute because I was too worried. I'd send messages to people on Facebook and then worry that I'd come across as a twat. I went on play dates with people that I had nothing in common with and haven't seen since.

Yet, as I became a regular at a particular mother and toddler group, I realized that I had started to look forward to going. That there were four mums there who I'd started to feel a bit more comfortable with. We started to meet up for play dates outside the official group, we then met up one evening for a few drinks without children. At this point we knew that there was no going back (and by that, I mean to the mother and toddler group), we'd formed a 'clique', and do you know what? It felt good!

It's a bit like dating really. You have to go through some horrific first dates before you get a good one. Everyone is well behaved for the first couple of dates and then facades start to fall until you end up a married couple loving each other warts and all.

I don't clean my house for them, I don't necessarily even shower before I see them. I don't pretend to be the perfect mother in front of them and at least one of my children has permanently scarred one of theirs. We have danced until four together, been on weekends away together. We had one particular night out where I was home by 9:45 pm and didn't recover for a good two days. We've cancelled play dates at the last minute because we've been so hungover, we've had to stop en route to be sick (no names mentioned). But, after all these times not once have I thought, *I hope they don't think I'm a dick*. Not once have I worried that they might judge me or think I'm a terrible mother or say, 'aren't her children rough' or 'the little one is a bit clingy isn't he!' Or 'I can't believe she forgot nappies, wipes, spare clothes and snacks again!'. They love me and my children...Like family.

I would love to know how many hours of my life I've spent crouched on the floor of a toilet watching someone else (mostly my children) do their business.

The above thought came to me fairly recently as I excused myself from the table to take one of my children to the toilet for what felt like the 147th time. We were out for lunch with a big group of friends of which I am the only one with three children, no nappies and no husband to help. The boys had had squash (bloody exciting day out) and therefore their need for the toilet had multiplied tenfold. In all honesty I was contributing so little to the conversation that there was no point in me being there. When I did contribute, I offered the above thought and I'm pretty sure they all thought there was no point in me being there either.

As a side note, I am that friend. The friend who at social occasions spends her time entertaining the children so that the parents can have a good time. They think I'm an excellent mother but actually it's because I have limited adult conversation but can talk about spider man/Andy's magic clock/Spirit the horse (despite the fact my children only watch the Spanish version) for hours and therefore enjoy being hero worshipped by small children.

The first thing I do when I know someone is popping over is heavily bleach the downstairs loo whilst spraying

Dettol All in One Disinfectant Spray (not an ad) like its air freshener to try and disguise the smell of urine. It's not that I have a dirty house, in fact I would say I'm slightly OCD (I get if from my mother) it's just that the moment I clean the loo one of the boys goes for a wee and pees all over the toilet seat, down the sides of the toilet, on the wall, on the skirting board and on the floor. Basically, they wee anywhere but in the toilet despite the fact I've put a ping pong ball with a smiley face down there to make it fun! I've also noticed recently that rather than pulling their trousers down to their knees, so they have control over direction they simply pull their trousers down so their willy rests on the waist band and close their eyes aiming in the general direction of the loo and failing miserably! I have a shoes off rule in the house but would firmly encourage people to put their shoes back on again to use the loo.

I have brought up three fiercely independent young men so far. They couldn't possibly hold my hand to cross a road or let me help them put on their shoes when we're running ten minutes late already. They wouldn't dream of letting me help them brush their teeth or choose their outfits, so they don't look like they got dressed in the dark after raiding a Hobo's wardrobe. Oh no. But they do all like me to crouch in front of them and hold their knees whilst they go for a poo. They use these opportunities to ask one of life's great questions like, 'where do babies come from?' Or 'why do you have hair sticking out your nose?' They don't allow anyone else to do the knee holding and none of them to my knowledge have ever done a poo at Pre-School or School. I should feel honored that as long as I am there, holding their knees they can poo, but I have realised that that is the only condition. A toilet and toilet role are not essentials. They are happy to lay one out pretty much anywhere as long as I am there crouching with them holding their knees.

Thank God I have dogs and therefore always have a poo bag somewhere on my person. Thank God I know what leaves will leave a rash/sting or simply just spread because this knowledge has proved invaluable on many an occasion. On one trip to Sandringham (yes, the Queen's Norfolk home) Baby Number One needed a poo. We had just cracked Potty training, we were too far from the public loos to get there even at a sprint. I won't go into gruesome details but there is a vital detail we missed. There are no bins at Sandringham.

Ah, Potty training. The three consecutive years where the phrases: 'Do you need a wee?', 'Shall we try for a wee wee?', 'Is there a wee wee coming?', 'No? Well, I think there is because I can see it coming out', 'Shall we try sitting on the Potty? No? The big boy toilet? No? A wild wee? Well, we shouldn't really, I don't think the neighbors want you wee weeing outside their house.' These were repeated 17,000 times a day! I got so fed up with hearing myself saying them yet couldn't seem to stop.

In hindsight I think I had quite an easy time Potty training. All of them wanted to do it and it never felt like too much of a battle. Obviously, my washing pile felt infinite because they'd go through seven outfits a day. It wouldn't just be their pants and trousers that got wet either but their socks and tops too! How? And I'm sure we can't be the only house where you get a waft of stale wee when you sit down on the living room carpet even though Potty training finished a year ago.

I also remember all the conflicting advice. Unwanted advice is part and parcel of being a parent, but I remember feeling like everyone wanted to have their say on how I should Potty train my children. Put a nappy on for a nap, don't put a nappy on for a nap, don't leave the house, wait until the Summer and let them run around naked, make sure you always put them in pants so they can feel when they are wet, don't reward them, use chocolate to reward them, don't tell them off for having an accident, go ballistic when they have an accident and then this complete knob at singing group who felt it important to tell me that she thought Potty training my children this young would give them toileting issues for life! Images of the Daily Mail story rushed through my mind: *Mother uses Potty to decapitate busy body whilst singing The Wheels on the Bus.*

The only time I can remember feeling really stressed was when I was still new to the school run with Baby Number One and Baby Number Three at sixteen months would no longer wear a nappy. I kid you not, I would put it on him, he would rip it off. I would have to physically restrain him with my arms and legs to attempt to put the nappy on with my teeth (this is NOT and exaggeration) and so I gave in. We started Potty training. I would say I'm fairly chilled out and so him weeing all over my house, fine. Taking several outfit changes to baby groups, fine. Him weeing all over me in the pick-up line, not so fine. Not only was I fucking freezing as the warm wee went cold, but he was too and making this known in the only way he knew how (loudly). But I was also aware I smelt like piss. This was not one of the first impressions I wanted to make with the mums and dads in the line who I would be queuing with for the next seven years.

It's okay though, I became best friends with the other two ladies in the line who were also holding their toddlers like bombs and stank of piss. We don't always smell of piss, but we do still treat our children like unexploded bombs!

The Affair

What a title for a chapter! Who has already started thinking, *what a bastard, I can't believe he cheated on her when she was pregnant / had just had a baby / generally?* In which case, why the presumption it was him? Why did you not think it could be me? I can definitely fit clandestine sex into my day, I just don't bloody want to!

I should clarify…My husband was not having an affair. My hormones however totally convinced me that he was. I was over at my mum's (it takes a village to raise a baby and all that) bathing baby number one and two. I turned to her and tearfully explained that I thought my husband was having an affair. "Why?" she asked. "What happened?" Absolutely nothing had happened, he had as he has always been, my absolute rock. But, at that moment I was totally convinced. The feeling didn't last long, the hormone surge passed, and I forgave his affair.

I used to be an avid EastEnders watcher. Having children put paid to that, I can barely focus on an episode of Peppa Pig let alone the goings on in Walford! However, I remember one story line in particular back in 1999…Jackie Owen had a relationship with Gianni Di Marco (who I fancied like mad). She had serious PMT, and her foul moods and violent temper made her an absolute nightmare to be with. Well, I am Jackie Owen and my husband Gianni Di Marco!

This is a massive exaggeration, I do have horrific moods linked to my hormones, but I don't have the violent temper. My husband and I have been together for fourteen years now. We met on the first day of the first term of our first year at university and despite me being too drunk to remember our first kiss he very kindly took me to the doctors the following day for an anti-sickness injection (in my bottom) and has put up with me ever since.

For this he deserves a Sainthood! The more perceptive among you will have noted that I cry...A lot. This was not the case before I got pregnant (unless I was drunk). I remember watching 'Surprise, Surprise' pregnant with Baby Number One sobbing as much as I did the first time, I watched Armageddon (when Bruce Willis and Ben Affleck touch hands through the glass!) I refused to go on holiday with my in-laws whilst pregnant with Baby Number Two because my boobs were too big, and I looked inappropriate in all the bikinis I tried on. You'll be pleased to know that once my hormones and I had calmed down, I did go. Whilst pregnant with Baby Number Three I had an absolute wobbler on the way to a fourth birthday party. We were late. I hadn't got a present. When we should have been arriving at the party, we were driving in the wrong direction to get a present. Then I couldn't find the pen (a new one I'd had to purchase for the occasion) to write the card and well I lost the plot...With Baby Number One and Baby Number Two sat in the back of the car I proceeded to have what my husband later described as a tantrum. He asked me to stop crying/screaming/swearing or get out of the car. I obviously chose to get out of the car. He drove off laughing at me sweating profusely at him in the rear view mirror. But what neither of us realised was that because of roadworks he wouldn't be able to pull in for half a mile. I began the walk heavily pregnant and fuming. When I finally reached the car, I was still heavily pregnant but now slightly sheepish. We arrived an hour late to the two-hour party. Baby Number One told anyone that would listen that, "Mummy was really cross because she couldn't find a pen." You could see all those mummies and daddies catching each other's eyes. I hope they were thinking of an occasion they'd experienced something similar rather than thinking, *what a bloody psycho...She's just like Jackie Owen.*

Only once did my husband threaten divorce. We were going to one of his oldest and my best friend's weddings. I'd been out of the house for three hours having my hair put up for the occasion. I am one of those people that never has the balls to complain. Feed me undercooked, over seasoned food in a restaurant, 'yum delicious!', Corked wine? 'My favourite', someone drives into the back of me at a roundabout. "Please don't worry, it was my fault." I am one of them! So, I had my hair done. I looked like an eighty's bride. It was horrific. "Thank you so much, I love it!" I get home, he knows me well and doesn't say anything. I go to the bathroom and start ripping out curbi grips. "I'm not bloody coming!" I shout. An hour later he gets in the car. "If you don't come, I will divorce you!"

"Fuck off! I'm not bloody coming!" He leaves. Cue total devastation. I did go, I left ten minutes later with my hair in a 'Mum bun'.

After Baby Number Three I struggled with post-partum thyroiditis. This is a condition caused by the thyroid becoming inflamed after you give birth. It happens to a small number of women about 6 months after giving birth. The symptoms include: Anxiety and irritability, mood swings, difficulty sleeping, feeling tired all the time, loss of interest in sex and weight loss. Yes, that's right everything you'd expect after having a baby. But I also felt ill all the time. I'd have blinding migraines and sickness which left me unable to look after the boys. I had to rely heavily on my mum and dad. Eventually my husband got so fed up with me constantly retiring to bed at the weekends that he made me go to the doctors. It was a relief to find out that it wasn't just my hormones. There had been moments where I'd felt so rough that I'd given myself weeks to live (I belong on the stage). By the time I had been to the doctors, had blood tests, got said test results, got referred to the specialist, had an ultrasound on my thyroid and had further blood tests, my thyroid had sorted itself out. I was back to my 'normal' hormonal self. I would like to add that I found having an ultrasound and not seeing a baby an extremely strange experience. However, as the sonographer pointed out it would be an even stranger experience to be growing a baby in your neck!

"Oh, Bloody Hell, I've forgotten Their Bloody Shoes!"

Travelling with children is not easy. You do anything to make your packing lighter and life a bit simpler. That is why when we go on holiday to somewhere hot, I only take sandals for the boys. No socks, no trainers, no laces just slip-on sandals and it works, they can put them on and take them off independently, they don't smell, and I don't have to try and find matching pairs of socks (a rare find in this house!)

The last few times we've been away we have left the house in the early hours and caught early morning flights. The bags are left by the front door for my husband to put in the car. The boys' clothes to get changed into at the airport are folded carefully and placed into hand luggage. Their sandals left on top of the shoe cupboard to put on them as we leave the house. It's this final crucial step I forgot. Halfway to Birmingham Airport and I'm straightening out all those little niggles in my head: I definitely turned the emersion off, didn't I? Did I turn off the straighteners? Yep, I packed them! Have we got the passports? Did I check they were still in date? Have I packed jumpers for the flight? Yes, yes, I have but oh bloody hell, I've forgotten their shoes!

So, there we are at Birmingham Airport. I've managed to find some snowshoes in the boot that fit Baby Number Two but the other two are shoeless. Baby Number Three can sit in the push chair and is therefore not too noticeable, but Baby Number One had to walk through Birmingham Airport in his bare feet. He then (because we were late) had to climb onto the aero plane in bare feet, then walk across the runway at Lanzarote in bare feet, through Lanzarote airport in bare feet and well you get the idea! My husband had almost forgiven my packing incompetence until we walked back in our own front door to see those three pairs of sandals lined up on the shoe cupboard.

I have realised since starting this chapter that all the travelling stories I have to share with you are actually a direct result of my own actions rather than the children!

Why were we late for our flight to Lanzarote? Well for two reasons really. Firstly, I thought it was necessary to pack the boys' scooters for our week's holiday. It turns out they made the suitcases too heavy, and we had to empty and repack them at the check in desk before we could be charged a fortune to take them. Secondly, my hand luggage was full of things to keep the boys entertained on the flight. This included Lego encased in a washing tablet tub. Security did not like this tub and sent it for another x-ray. This would not have been an issue if we weren't already running late due to 'scooter-gate'. But as I stood in the queue I turned to my husband. "You better take the boys and go," I said with tears in my eyes. He rolled his in return and off he went down to our gate. The Lego and I made that flight…Just!

My husband and I had decided that we weren't going to go on any more holidays that included a flight after taking baby numbers one and two to Croatia. On that occasion all four of us nearly missed our flight. I've often wondered how people miss their flights once they've been booked in. I'd listen to, 'this is the last call for Mrs Jones' and wonder what the hell Mrs Jones could be doing. Well, let me tell you Mrs Jones has probably taken baby Jones to change his nappy. She'll have arranged to meet Mr Jones and their toddler outside the toilet and Mr Jones will indeed go to meet her. What neither Mr nor Mrs Jones realise is that when they arranged this meeting point, they were talking about different toilets. We made that flight; still married…Just!

We almost got divorced before we had even left. With three days to go before our holiday my husband suggested that I should get all the passports together. No problem I think, I keep them all in the document file with all the other important things. I take out the bulging document file and find three passports. Baby Number One's is nowhere to be seen. I didn't panic simply checked the other places in the house that I keep important documents: The cupboard in the kitchen that we keep glasses in, the bottom of the cupboard in my room, 'my drawer' in the kitchen etc. I found £100 in cash which had been given to one of the boys on their baptism but no bloody passport.

I begin to panic! I empty my cupboard, the cupboard under the stairs, the document box. Nothing. I google 'emergency replacement passports for children', not possible! I tell my husband…He goes mental! I message all members of my immediate family asking them to come over and rip the house apart to look for it. Within twelve minutes of being there my sister-in-law finds the passport. It was in the document box; it had got caught in my husband's new work contract. Now who's bloody fault is it?

Summer holidays in my childhood were spent camping. My parents would load up the car, the roof rack, and the trailer. The seven of us would head off for four weeks. We would drive as far afield as Portugal and pitch up our tents. My fondest memories are of holidays in the South of France. We spent our days by the Ardeche River, kayaking, jumping off rocks, my mum would sunbathe topless (which at the time was gross but now I would take my hat off to her because after three children have gnawed at my boobs there is zero chance of this happening).

We still holiday together. Every other year the whole family go away together for a week. This year we are off to Tuscany, all twenty-six of us! I am actually writing this chapter from Tuscany, our little family of five are having a week's peace and quiet before the chaos begins in five days' time. We will spend our evenings drunkenly retelling the best stories from our childhood holiday. My sister particularly likes to tell of the time I nearly drowned her. We were playing in the rapids of the Ardeche River. Mum and Dad were watching us proudly from the bank. We got caught in said rapid and started to fight against it rather than letting it carry us to slower water all of three feet away. We began to scream for help. "Look what a lovely time they're having," said Mum to Dad. I began to climb on my sister, pushing her under water. "Look at how much they love each other," said my dad to my mum. At that point, my sister with her last ounce of oxygen nailed me in the nose with her elbow. I let go of her and we drifted down the river to safety.

We unintentionally got our parents back later that holiday. We discovered the air pocket under our dinghy and spent hours playing underneath it. A Dutch couple canoeing past saw the upturned dinghy and began shouting to the shore. Mum and Dad at last looked up from their book/boobs and saw their children's dinghy floating upside down with no sign of their children. Ha! That will teach them to relax and enjoy themselves!

Our most recent holiday to Italy ended up with me carrying one toddler, two car seats and a backpack across Rome Ciampino Airport all whilst dragging a suitcase whilst encouraging my two older boys to carry their bags and a car seat in forty-degree heat because we were late for our flight home. We'd got stuck in traffic, used the wrong pin on the credit card whilst filling up with fuel and if I'm honest? Left too late. My husband told me to go with the boys and catch the flight because we couldn't afford replacement tickets for all of us. I don't think we'd really thought it through. By the time I arrived at check in I was a crying, sweating mess. The heavy suitcase I had pulled all that way was in his name so I couldn't check in and I had started to wonder whether I was competent enough to manage these three crying children not just on a plane but on arrival and back to the car park. Anyway, my children and I sat/lay on the cold tile floor having been told we had fifteen minutes before we would miss our flight. In swans my husband all smiles and charming to the lady behind the desk. I could have killed him…He'd only had to wheel one suitcase! I also think he was slightly disappointed that he hadn't manage to wangle a childfree (and wife free) flight home.

It's not just travelling abroad that is made more difficult with children it is travelling in general. I'm not a fan of driving. I don't find it enjoyable or relaxing, quite the opposite in fact. It took me five years and nine attempts to pass my driving test. I can't remember all the reasons why I didn't pass (can't say failed) but on my worst try I was driven back to the test centre for going right at a roundabout. I can't parallel or reverse park and always aim for a drive through space (if you know, you know). I never use car parks with a ticket barrier because stopping close enough to get your ticket is way too stressful! One of the best things about having children is that I can use the parent and baby parking, they are bigger, spaced further apart and therefore I have a higher chance of getting the car in between the white lines. What proves even more difficult is getting the children in the car to go anywhere. Nipping to the shops or around to my mum's is a logistical nightmare. I thought it would get easier as they got older. No carrying heavy car seats with screaming babies, no spending all journey looking in the rearview mirror at the mirror which shows the screaming baby's reflection. But no, now we have arguments about who is sitting on which car seat, on which side of the car. We have arguments about what we are going to be listening to on the radio. We have arguments about whether the windows should be up or down, the air-conditioning higher or lower, whether Mummy clipped that cars wing mirror or not. I long for the days when I could just turn up the radio and drown out the screaming baby.

Long journeys are the worst though. We only travel at bedtime now because otherwise I think I would genuinely have driven the car off a ravine. I know a lot of people find electronic devices work. They didn't for us. When they were really little, they were more trouble than they were worth. 'It's not working!', 'I've turned it off by accident!', 'What do I press now?', 'Mummy! Muuuuummmmyyy! MUUUUUMMMMYYYY!' So we stopped using them. We don't know whether they'd work now because my husband drove off with them on the roof of the car. We never discovered them, nor have we replaced them. Now we do it old-school: We listen to audiobooks and play I-Spy. And that is why we only travel at nighttime when they are asleep.

The other issue with long journeys during the day is the need for a pit stop. A well-planned pit stop at a National Trust place on route can be good fun but tends to add an extra hour to your journey. A service station on the motorway with three children is hell!

I do a lot of solo travelling. We often meet my husband at our final destination. He travels by train from work...I know the lucky bastard! Solo parenting in a service station put me off daytime travelling forever! I was travelling south to my in-laws, it's a five-hour trip and so I stopped halfway at a service station. I got the children fed and watered and feeling rather smug took them all to the toilet. Baby Number Three was safely in a baby sling, Baby Number Two and Baby Number One were on reins. Baby Number One by this point was desperate for the loo and extremely vocal about it but I could not maneuver all four of us into the loo to be able to help him. A very kind lady offered to hold Baby Number Two's reins for me whilst I sorted it. Job done. I then really needed to go to the loo. Could she I asked to hold the baby for me whilst I went to the loo? As I handed my baby over to her, I had that sudden panic…What happens if she runs off with my baby whilst I'm weeing. Could she I ask just stand in front of the open door holding my baby whilst I did a wee? Brilliant I thought as I went to pull my trousers down. Oh, bollocks I thought as I realised I was wearing a jump suit. I hope that that lady reads this and realises how grateful I was to her that day and how sorry I am that she had to watch me wee naked.

We have holidays planned now as just the four of us. I'm excited and nervous about it in equal parts. One of me, three of them. I look forward to telling you all about it.

He's a Biter...

I truly believe that if my children woke up to find me dead on the sitting room floor, they would use my corpse as a trampoline before arguing over who got to eat which part of me for breakfast!

I often turn up at my mum and dad's exhausted whilst the boys are still running around like Tasmanian Devils and sigh. "I wish I had three girls." Their reply is always the same. "They wouldn't be any different, they are your children after all!"

We're a physical family, both my husband and I are good at sport, both of us love the outdoors and so do the boys. The boys are at their happiest outside with space to run, climb and make a lot of noise. They will happily run, climb, and make a lot of noise in the house but it always ends in tears (usually mine). Until recently my children were incapable of sitting down and playing. We have just reached a point where they might sit down for fifteen minutes to build Lego or Duplo before they take off again. Arts and crafts activities last ten minutes and yet seem to take ten hours to set up and pack away.

To retain my sanity, I went out. My husband soon realised that this was the only way and his pleas to 'just stay at home and have a chilled one' were silenced. It is not unusual for us to have done a dog walk, activity, swim, and shop by lunchtime at a weekend! We recently had friends who are expecting their first come and stay. It was a rainy weekend and by Sunday Morning the house was a mess and the children quite literally climbing the walls. With the promise of nice cake and coffee we took them to our local soft play. I've mentioned that it was a rainy weekend, haven't I? Therefore, every other family with young children in a ten-mile radius had also descended on soft play. Our friends hated it. You could see them looking at each other making a silent promise never to come to one of these places with their unborn child. It didn't help when one of their wedding rings got lost in the ball pit whilst coming down a surprisingly fast slide (we did find it). I can assure you, they now frequent soft plays with their son.

Soft plays get a bad press. They really are like a living hell on earth and yet we all go to them. I remember crawling around a soft play after a toddler whilst breast feeding a baby looking at those parents whose children were big enough to get on with it by themselves who were enjoying a hot coffee and sit down and being desperate to emulate this. I haven't for one reason. My children are biters.

Back them into a corner and they bite, lie on top of them so they feel trapped, and they bite, look at them a bit funny and they bite. This is a bit of an exaggeration because Baby Number One was not a biter, he was a shover. He especially loved to push over little girls. This was not ideal but definitely preferable to biting. Baby Number Two was not what I would call a serial biter, but he has been known to do it. One of the very first play dates I went on with another Pre

School family ended up in a bite. I am now really good friends with the Mum, and she has forgiven Baby Number Two but when it happened, I was absolutely mortified. Fortunately, it wasn't a 'bad bite' – teeth marks but no blood or long-lasting bruise. Baby Number Three however is an absolute fucking nightmare when it comes to biting. He's never bitten a complete stranger but that's about as good as it gets. When he goes for it, he really goes for it, and we've had several incidents where I haven't got their quick enough and he's basically bitten down to the bone!

So, have I ever sat on a sofa and drunk coffee whilst my children play? Absolutely not! What I have done is chased after them, sweating like a pig, knocking other people's children flying ready to throw myself between Baby Number Three and his next victim!

As they grow up the boys are definitely more aware of who is up for physical play and who isn't and tend to gravitate towards those who can give as good as they get. I'm also pleased to report that even Baby Number Three seems to be growing out of biting, it now appears to only be his brothers who he will take a chunk out of, and they probably deserve it!

I still pick up from Pre School dreading the moment I have to sign the accident form because they've hurt someone. I think the staff there think I'm mad because I'm always so happy that they've been hurt and not the other way around.

The Calpol Kid

As a mother to three boys, with three years four months between the eldest and the youngest my life is spent in perpetual motion. They don't stop moving and normally at speed. Baby Number One walked at eleven months. We were delighted. Baby Number Two walked at ten months. We had our hands full. Baby Number Three walked at eleven months. We pushed him over. We were not ready for that yet!

Some accidents are unavoidable. We spend a lot of time outside: Walks, parks, scooter rides, playing in the garden. This is not because I am a firm believer in outdoor education, I am! It is because if we are in the house they climb the walls, quite literally! There is not a lamp they haven't broken, a curtain pole they haven't pulled down, a picture or painting sitting straight. And once, they've destroyed the house they turn on each other. Play fighting and wrestling soon turns into a thirst for blood! "Stop, it'll end in tears," I scream. It inevitably does but they still don't listen!

I wouldn't say I've been a regular in A & E, but I've been more times than I would have liked. We managed to make it to the day before Baby Number One's first birthday

71

before our first visit. I should mention that this doesn't include the very regular visits to our local GP with colds, temperatures, rashes and general grumpiness. At that point 4:45 am was a lie in. I don't know why we didn't just make him go back to sleep, didn't stick him in front of a screen, didn't lock him in a dark cupboard etc. but we didn't. We would take it in turns to go downstairs with him and watch the 'night screens' until 'Transworld' sport came on (we soon invested in Sky). It was Boxing Day, we were at my parents, Baby Number One was at an age that all he wanted to do was toddle so wouldn't stay in one room and be watched. He had to be followed wherever he went to prevent falling, choking, fingers in plug sockets etc. By eight am we'd been following this soon to be one year old around for over three hours. Then as he goes towards the stone steps that lead to the dining room, he bends in two at the tummy and head butts the step. Obviously, he screams and starts crying. I pick him up and look at the mark on his forehead, no blood, no bump but a definite dip. He's still screaming and then he's being sick. Next thing I know someone in the house has phoned 111 and they're sending an ambulance. Long story short? He was fine. The ambulance crew arrived and although confident there was nothing wrong had to take him in because he was so little. I looked like a mad lady in my Christmas pajamas and despite it being 8:30 am had been up for four hours so was exhausted. And then the worst thing happened. Two tired parents had not had the energy to change the nighttime nappy. We had silently agreed to wait for the inevitable post breakfast poo before doing so. As the ambulance lady picks him up, blue powdered gel falls through his pajama leg. I didn't know a nappy exploded if left for too long. The time to find out is not surrounded by health care professionals.

I learnt a lesson that day. The pediatric doctor who assessed our first born kindly told us we'd see a lot worse yet. He was right. Almost a year to the day later. Baby Number One, Baby Number Two, the dogs and I were on a walk. I had done what I always do and pushed the walk too far forgetting that my almost two-year-old had to turn around and walk back the same distance he had already travelled. Baby Number Two a matter of weeks old was safely tucked in the baby carrier. Baby Number One began to winge, and moan and my repertoire of songs was beginning to run dry. He was pulling on my hand; I wouldn't say being dragged but definitely propelled along when our hands slipped apart. He fell headfirst onto the only rock in a 100m radius. His head split open. Now, as a mother of three boys I have witnessed this, a fair few times but each time I am shocked by the amount of blood a forehead can pump out. So, there I am, half a mile from the car with two dogs, a baby in a carrier and a child spouting blood like a hose. You hear those stories about mothers lifting cars up unaided to save their child and I don't want to blow my own trumpet, but it was a little like that! He was soon glued back together again. Baby Number Two is yet to have a trip to A & E but the same cannot be said for Baby Number Three.

Accidents are unavoidable, take for example Baby Number Three jumping on a blow-up bed and swallow diving into the radiator. Despite his older brothers worries that, 'you can see his brain', 'his brain is leaking out!' He was soon glued back together and right as rain. The Mum guilt creeps in with these incidents but since there was literally nothing you could do about them even though you were right there you can tell it to bugger off. When an accident is avoidable that's when you allow the Mummy guilt to come and eat you alive for a while.

We'd just come back from two weeks holiday. There are suitcases, laundry, and holiday paraphernalia everywhere. My husband escaped to the driving range (I should have known then) and I was attempting to sort our lives out when I hear a shout from the sitting room. "Mummy, Baby Number Three is drinking the medicine." He couldn't deny it. He still had the Calpol bottle in his hand as I got into the room. That hospital visit was quite a difference experience. It was referred to as an accidental overdose. I was repeatedly asked questions about how much he had taken, where he had got it, how he had got the lid off. I couldn't answer any of them. I have no idea how much he'd drunk. There was 15ml left, and it hadn't been new. I had been distracted, busy sorting things out, not watching him. He had blood tests taken and a line fitted in case the blood test results showed he had too much paracetamol in his body. Between testing there was a four hour wait and as I sat there watching him have a bloody lovely time in the playroom I suddenly thought, *Shit! What if he isn't the only one of them to have drunk some?'* I face timed Baby Number Two and Baby Number One. My husband tried every tactic under the sun to try and get the truth out of them. Eventually, they conceded that they had helped him open it but hadn't drunk any. Little buggers! I'm still not sure if I believe them! After eight hours Baby Number Three was given the 'all clear'. He had not consumed a toxic amount. The Mum guilt ate me alive for days until I had a message from one of my oldest friends with three of her own. It read, 'Well done, you did so well to even notice. I'd have found an empty bottle of Calpol under the sofa a week later with absolutely no idea who had drunk it!'

I don't know if I'm the only mum to think this, but I quite like it if my children are a bit poorly. Not seriously poorly, thank goodness the worst that's come my way so far is a febrile convulsion. No, just a bit of a temperature or a sickness bug. My children don't sit still long enough to be mothered so I suppose it's my only chance! I'm always relieved when they bounce back the next morning though.

I talked in an earlier chapter about my NCT friend who later became Baby Number Three's Godmother. She and her husband are an inspiration to me not just as parents but their relationship, their resilience, and their positivity. Their beautiful boy Archie needed a heart transplant and when he was less than a year old was put on the waiting list at Newcastle Freeman's Hospital. His mummy moved to Newcastle to live in Ronald McDonald housing (thanks to all the loose change you give after eating your Maccy D's). His daddy stayed at their home in Worcestershire to carry on working. He would drive up to Newcastle every weekend to be with his family. I cannot do this story justice, I cannot even begin to imagine the ups and downs they went through as a family, the decisions they were asked to make, the sacrifices they made. It's a happy ending. Their beautiful boy got his new heart in October 2015 just as I was giving birth to Baby Number Two. He is now running circles around his parents. They have been through so much as a couple and when I shared my separation with them, they talked of how separation was a path they could have easily taken. They didn't. They took the harder path. I look at them and think why couldn't my husband take the hard path? Why did he give up when he felt the going get a bit rough? I hope that if I have the chance to have another relationship that it is more like theirs. That both of you are willing to give it everything they've got to make it work. I share this story with their permission because I want them to know what an inspiration they are, how proud I am to be their friend and in the hope that it will make you pause for a moment to think about organ donation, perhaps in a different light.

"Haven't You Got Your Hands Full?" "You Think?"

When people with young children tell me they're thinking about getting a dog I often impart the following wisdom. My dogs came first, and I love them almost as much as my children and therefore would never re home them, but I would never choose to get a dog post children if I knew how difficult it would be. Not until the children were old enough anyway!

Walking two dogs with three little boys is not the easiest and bizarrely enough it has got harder as they have got older. Picking up the baby carrier in our house gets the dogs more excited than if you wave a bone in their face. Part of my day with Baby Number One was to strap him in and walk for an hour. As he got bigger, he moved into a rucksack. Simple.

When I had a baby and a toddler, one would be carried and the other in the push chair. Simple. Unless of course the one in the push chair was losing their marbles because they didn't like blue, or the straps were strangling them (I'll show you strangling!)

When I had a baby, a toddler and a little boy walking the dogs became a logistical nightmare. It was less walking and more finding an open space to let them all run. I have had days where dog walks have left me in tears because nobody is fucking listening to me! Nobody comes when called, everyone heads off in their own direction and the toddler is trying to pick up poo! If it's not the children picking up poo it's the bloody dogs eating it! When Baby Number Two did his first poo on the Potty (it took some time) I did what all parents do and in an overly loud high pitched voice I ran upstairs to get Daddy. Daddy runs downstairs all excited to look at said poo (we no longer look at the poos) but there is no poo there just the dog licking her lips. I remember the health visitor telling me that it was good for children's immune systems to be around animals. As the dog affectionately licked my children faces later that day I remember thinking, *I don't think this is quite what she had in mind!*

'Do not let the dogs out!' Are words I say, shout, scream every time we leave the house. The school run is not necessarily a stress free time in our house and this is normally a result of me being totally ignored and the dogs being let out. Sometimes it's okay. Sometimes I can get them back in before they nearly get run over by our very patient neighbors. Sometimes they don't terrify other dog walkers by launching a commando-esque attack. However, there are occasions where they sense freedom and leg it so quickly bad things happen. Take for example the time I'm trying to round them up and all I can hear is a wailing noise. I run around the corner to see Tilly doing that excited wiggling action they do (if you know you know) jumping around a grandma who can only be described as a walking Roald Dahl illustration hunched over her walking frame feebly defending herself from this over excited puppy. Or the time I took the boys to feed the ducks and thought it would be a great idea to take the dogs for a run about too. The sun is shining, the boys and dogs run around the meadow, my husband and I smugly walk along holding hands. I take the boys over to the river to feed the ducks. We join the throngs of well-behaved middle-class families, all smiling at each other about the lovely day trip we are having when suddenly a black hound launches itself into the river, catching a duck in the process. The screams still echo around my head as the adults dived to cover their children's eyes, as they desperately tried to get their children away from the traumatizing situation. Then a voice screaming, 'leave it!' A voice I recognise. The voice of a man who is throwing himself into the river after the hound. That man nonchalantly clipping the lead on the hound is my husband. That hound is my dog. We slipped away unseen and will never go there again!

When we decided to have children, we decided not to 'try', we didn't talk about it, we just had a lot of sex! We had sex even when we didn't really want to be having sex. On one of these occasions, post work and shattered we were doing the deed. My husband on top when he begins to thrust wildly. *My God*, I thought, *where's he getting the energy, he is so into it!* I look up at him as he begins to make awful noises to accompany the wild humping. My husband is screaming and wildly humping because he is also being wildly humped…By the dog!

They are old ladies now. Quite happy with one walk a day as long as they are allowed to sleep on the sofas and lick the plates clean. They are (sorry if that grosses you out). There was a time when all the boys were little that they didn't have quite such a luxurious life. Yes, they'd get a long walk but then I'd have to shut them away (in a warm room listening to Radio four). I couldn't handle the mess on the floor whilst the boys crawled or the constant worry that the boys would poke their eyes or pull their tails and their reaction would be to snap. They were the wrong height for the boys, knocking the toddlers over, trying to lick the remnants of breakfast off their faces. It was all a bit much!

Now however, the boys, especially Baby Number One love nothing more than cuddling up on the sofa with them. We're past the stage of them chewing their toys or trying to sit on them all the time (that's dogs on children and children on dogs) and we live in a kind of dysfunctional harmony.

I dread the day that one of the dogs gets poorly. We had an insight into it recently and it was not pleasant. We'd been for a walk-in local woods. The boys will spend hours building dens there and Dog Number one will disappear for ages always popping back. When she came back this time though something was wrong. Her tail was between her legs, ears back and she was clearly 'spooked'. I presumed she'd had a run in with another dog/deer/cyclist, not ideal but not much I could do now. By the time we got home she was acting even more peculiarly. She wouldn't sit or move just stand in one position. She did this all night without eating, drinking, or going to the loo. I rang the vets the next morning and took her in. They explained that the most likely explanations were that she had damaged her spine or that she had a brain tumor which was showing itself for the first time. We had to leave her there. It hadn't been long since being left by my husband, the boys were so upset because they didn't want to leave her, and I was in pieces. Later that day we got a phone call. The vet had had a chance to thoroughly examine her, she'd had various scans and tests and the only thing they could find wrong was a slightly lame left leg. "Why is she behaving so oddly?" I asked. I read between the lines of the vets reply, "So what you are saying is that my dog is a hypochondriac?" That was indeed what the vet was suggesting.

All said and done I wouldn't be without them. Yes, they smell, yes sometimes I feel like I have five dependents who ignore everything I say but they are part of the family. Without them I wouldn't brave the outside every day no matter what the weather. Without them the boys and I would not have made so many amazing memories of streams we've played in, trees we've climbed, and secret gardens we've found. Without them my mental health after the birth of my babies would not have been so good. Without them I would find my evenings lonely and my house empty. Baby Number One worries that I will get lonely when they are with their dad and he finds it so reassuring that I will have the dogs for company. So, they are here to stay!

It's not a baby that breaks a marriage…Its sleep (or lack of it!)

They'll sleep longer if you give them a bottle of formula as their last feed.

They'll sleep longer if you prop their cot up at one end with the Bible.

They'll sleep longer once you have them eating solid food.

They'll sleep longer if you make them nap more in the day.

They'll sleep longer if you don't let them nap in the day.

They'll sleep longer if you rub tomato ketchup on their feet.

No! No, they won't sleep longer!

What is the world's obsession with how well your baby sleeps? Why does everyone feel the need to ask you? Why does it always seem to become a competition where everyone either wants to have the baby that sleeps the most (so they can be smug) or the baby that sleeps the least (so they can be a survivor)?

My children are early risers, always have been. It's a bit of a killer but it also means they go to bed early enough for me to have a bit of an 'evening' which I will take. When friends hear about their early morning wake ups, they often say, "Why don't you put them to bed later, then they'll get up later." Well, 'friend' I'll tell you why...Because if I put them to bed an hour later, they will still wake as the cockerel crows but will wake in a foul mood because they've had an hours less sleep. They will behave like devil twats for the rest of the day, or worse, they will have a danger nap and I won't be able to get them to bed until my bedtime meaning I've lost all my evening. At this point they don't tend to press their point much further.

Might I also add that we have tried lots of different ways of trying to get our children to stay in bed until a reasonable hour. The Gro Clock for example was one of our purchases. Known to work for so many with rave reviews there are several reasons it did not work in our house:

1. The Gro Clock is in the child's bedroom. The child is in the parents' bedroom. It defeats the object of said Gro Clock if the parent has to get out of bed to take the child to see whether the Sun has indeed come up. By the time this has been established the parent is up and might as well stay up.

2. The child cannot sleep with the Gro Clock because he feels like the stars are 'watching him' and therefore doesn't want to sleep in their bedroom anymore.

3. The child realises that if he presses the button on the side of the clock at any point then the Sun will come up. The parents' realised that they preferred the child climbing into bed with them and going to sleep rather than waking the whole house at two o'clock in the morning because the bastard Sun has come up!

With Baby Number One I religiously got out of bed each time he woke and fed him in the armchair next to the bed. I would then put him back in his basket with the same careful technique as one might use whilst handling a bomb. Normally he'd wake just as my body relaxed into the mattress and then the process would start again.

My husband tried too but it's true what they say...Men don't have that innate sense women do about babies being in bed with them. When Baby Number One was about sixteen weeks old we were staying at my parents. Baby Number One was supposed to be sleeping in my old cot (new mattress, no bumpers before you judge) but he just wasn't sleeping. I was exhausted, I kept trying to feed him, but he was doing the pull your nipple so hard with toothless gums move and I'd hit a brick wall. My husband took over and I fell into a deep sleep. Until…THUD…WAAAAAAAA…'OH MY GOD!' Yes, you would be right in thinking that Baby Number One had gone to sleep on my husband's chest. My husband had also gone to sleep (I don't blame him, we were knackered) and rolled over throwing Baby Number One to the floor. He was fine! My husband and I weren't!

We threw money at the problem, many desperate, early morning Amazon orders of Ewan the Dream Sheep, swaddling blankets, white noise monitors. They didn't work. Then at about four months old he found his thumb. By five months old I would put him down for his nap/for bed after a feed and he'd get himself to sleep. This carried on for about four months, I returned to work and there were some mornings my husband had to wake him to take him to nursery. Nailed it! Or so we thought. Baby Number One is six years old and still doesn't sleep through the night (not every night anyway) AND as a result of our amazon purchases can only fall asleep to audio books! Nightmare!

When you have babies close together, sleeping becomes a matter of survival. Before the arrival of Baby Number Two we splashed out on a 'Next to Me' crib. One that connects to the bed, you can drop the side to make feeding easy but keep baby safe etc. I don't think Baby Number Two went in it much, but it was great for keeping my water bottle, phone, book and necessary baby paraphernalia in for easy reach. Sometimes I would genuinely feel that I had been feeding my baby all night. Just switching sides so I wouldn't wake up all lopsided.

My husband and I shared duties at this point. We would have Baby Number Two in our bed and then when Baby Number One (21 months by now) woke he would be taken to the spare room, so everyone got a bit of sleep. When Baby Number Three came along we kept up the pretense of having the 'Next to Me' crib but co-sleeping had become the best way to ensure anyone in the house got some sleep. I can safely say it was not good for our marriage.

I still wake sometimes panicking, ripping off the duvet and searching the bed for my baby. I normally find them but now their fully formed little boys!

I am of the genuine belief that you either get a sleeper or you don't! I didn't! I don't get asked for advice about raising children very often (bizarre, I know). If I do, I normally explain that following my lead may result in them being as sleep deprived as I have been. I occasionally get asked if I wished I had done sleep training. The 'cry it out' or the one where you slowly move out the room. The answer is no. I hate the sound of my children crying, I've already admitted to giving in to their every whim and honestly? I like sleeping with them. I love how much they need me and love me, and I know that in a few years' time they won't be sneaking into my bed and stealing my duvet and I will miss them. Yes, there are some nights where I feel like accidentally pushing them out of bed because they're snoring or star fishing but instead, I take my pillow and lie across the bottom of the bed. They are so little that no one's feet can find me there.

I sometimes wonder whether if I had done 'sleep training' with my brood would my marriage have survived? My husband worked hard, commuted a long way and it made sense for him to sleep in the spare room but if my children had slept through all night and he had slept in the same bed as me, would it have stopped him leaving? Of course, if bloody wouldn't! He left me for such bigger reasons. But if I hadn't done it this way, I would have spent my days as a tired wretch who couldn't parent their way out of a paper bag.

When you have your third baby the power balance switches...

I will always maintain that going from zero to one baby is the hardest and then as you have more it gets easier. Actually, I take it back, I don't think it gets easier I think you lower your expectations and accept that you're going to do a piss poor job but it's okay because it will be the same for all of them!

I remember receiving a card from some of my parents' friends who wrote, 'congratulations on the birth of Baby Number Three, what a gorgeous name, but beware the power balance has now shifted'. I didn't know what they meant, and I remained in the dark for the first few months at least.

This is going to sound arrogant...But that's okay because it is! I bossed being a mum of three in those early days. There was not a group I didn't attend, not a walk I couldn't do, no lack of sleep I would complain about. Baby Number Three was fed, wrapped up and put in the baby carrier where he would stay until he needed feeding again or had done a shit. Those were the days because as soon as Baby Number Three realised there was more to life than walk and sleep the power balance did indeed shift.

Even now my Baby Number One will admonish his little brothers. "Remember, Mummy only has two hands!" And this is the truth! Two hands, two hips, two knees seem to be the sticking points. I can only carry two children (although have been known to put one on my shoulders and one on each hip for short distances. However, it is very dangerous, and I wouldn't recommend it. There is no chance of saving the child falling off your shoulders without throwing one or both of the other children to the ground). I am not of big stature and therefore cannot sit all three children on my knee. There is always one left out and it is always the one who screams the quietest. I only have two arms so can only give two children cuddles. There is always one left out and you've got it, it's the one who screams the quietest. I can only hold two hands to walk across the road. There is always one left out, the one who screams the loudest and therefore quite frankly I could do without!

The worst feeling in the world is that you are not enough for your children. That is a feeling I live 90% of the time (even when they are sleeping, I can only lie next to two of them). They would all like my full attention all the time and are therefore missing out all the time. However, there are moments when they do not need me at all and they play with each other beautifully, without ripping each other's hair out. These times do not come that often but every time they do, I am so grateful to have three children born so close together. I often see it on holiday, when others go looking for friends to play with my little tribe have everything they need right there! They are so happy with each other as playmates. Then one of them gauges the others eye out and I go back to wishing I'd sewn up my vagina after one!

The worst thing about having three children is those moments when you lose control. When you take your eye of them in the park to marvel in the beauty of the world and then realise that you now have one child wandering in the car park, one dangling by a leg from the monkey bars and one shitting in the sand pit. Which would you attend first? Your favorite obviously!

My parents have five children, and we have a lot of banter about who the favorite is. I don't know why because we all know it's my eldest brother. Mum and Dad barely deny it now! They always say, "Our favorite is the one who needs us most." I am the complete opposite. My favorite varies day to day and is always the one who needs me the least. The least whingy, the least clingy, the least violent and the one who doesn't want to play pirates. I hate playing pirates, mostly because I'm shit at it. I put on a hat, make a hook out of a finger and in a tired voice say, "Argh, me hearties!" That is it, that's all I've got!

I cannot wait to see their relationships develop. Already you can see them looking out for each other and making sure none of them are left behind when they go off adventuring. I am immensely proud of them and the way they look after each other and enjoy each other.

I am not necessarily looking forward to their teenage years. That funny smell teenage boys' rooms have, finding socks under the bed, body odor and hormones and the inevitable fights. Recently the boys had supper with their cousins at my mum and dad's house. When Dad dropped them off, they were full of the stories that he had been telling them around the table:

- Their two big uncles fighting and their Uncle D ringing the police claiming Uncle B was trying to kill him. By the time the police arrived the boys were both bored, had finished trying to kill each other and had moved on to another game.
- The time Uncle B shot Uncle D in the bottom with his air rifle from his bedroom window. An excellent shot of a moving target and perhaps one of the reasons that he joined the army.
- When Uncle B had his request for a sit on lawn mower rejected and so decided to create one with the petrol lawn mower, a booster seat and rope. Ingenious, no? What was ingenious was him using his littlest brother as the guinea pig.

I have so many wonderful memories of adventures with my brothers and sister: Bike rides, picnics, tree houses, laser tag, murder in the dark, putting on plays and then crying because the boys took the piss, epic Sylvanian family set ups that the boys would attack with their Playmobil. I can remember playing Peter Pan. We had a spinning table in our bedroom and the boys would spin it as fast as they could whilst my sister and I jumped off it in the hope we'd fly...We didn't, and it did result in a fractured wrist.

I don't really remember the fights we used to have (although I know we used to have them, I have the scars!) However, I do remember as a teenager flushing my sister's top down the toilet because she wouldn't let me wear it! I also remember my big brother ruining my first time in a night club by dragging me outside and ringing my dad. To be fair I was only fifteen at the time, but I didn't speak to him for weeks. I snogged a few of his mates to get even if I remember correctly!

I can't help but think that my three boys have got so much fun coming their way!

Having three children in three years, three months has its challenges. But I think having one child, or five, or two with ten years apart has its own challenges too. I always knew it was what I wanted because it was what I had known and loved, and I am grateful that I was able to do it for them and for me.

Did You Not See It Coming?

The honest answer to that? No! I knew that he wasn't happy, that his commute had become too much, that he was spending more time in London, but did I ever think he would leave me? No!

Looking back, I can see that I'd been walking on eggshells. I was doing anything I could to try and make him happier: 'Yes, stay in London I'm fine', 'you want to play golf this weekend despite the fact we haven't seen you all week...Of course', 'you want to delay our family holiday with friends so you can go to Marbella with people I don't know to play golf? Go for it!' As he pulled away, I tried desperately to keep him close. I'd hold his hand for him to shrug it away, go for a cuddle for him to turn away, I bought lingerie, shaved my legs, pulled out all the stops but was gutted every time I didn't get the physical affection I needed.

When he first started commuting, we'd speak several times a day, he would always come home to sleep even if it was only to see the boys for five minutes in the morning. Towards the end of our relationship, I would get one worded replies by message, and he would spend most nights in London. I can see how the commute caused the distance between us. He would often leave before any one was awake, he would come home to the house in darkness, food to be warmed up on the side and a night in the spare room because the boys were in our bed. I look back and think I should have stayed up later, done better sleep training with the boys but I didn't. Not because I didn't love my husband but because I was looking after three children under the age of four by myself. If I hadn't have gone to bed early, if I'd done more sleep training then I would have been even more tired, too tired to function? Probably not but too tired to be the best parent I can be? Yes.

He didn't say anything, obviously I asked. I had no idea it had become such a problem. I spend my days with other mums, people in the same situation as me. For me our relationship was normal, we had three young children. We had made the decision to live where we live so that he could go to work for long hours, and I'd have the support of my family. Life was about our children, I lost myself to motherhood. I was so happy in my role as mummy and so happy as a family of five that I presumed (wrongly) that he was as happy. On the other hand, he saw us living two completely different lives. He realised that he was happier with his life in London, with a job that gave him satisfaction. He decided that although he loved me as the mother of his children, he was no longer in love with me and therefore ended our marriage.

He had decided all of this without talking to me and I think that is what I found so hard. When he had reached the conclusion that he wanted to separate and told me it was too late for discussion, for counselling, for questions even. He left and didn't want to talk about it anymore.

This happened in the September, just after our return from Italy. My family had all noticed a change in his behavior but by then it was the norm for me. His need for time alone, his lack of interest in anything I had to say, having to look after the children alone even though he was there. I carried on as normal presuming this was a rut we'd get out of. Thinking that we were still together, still having sex and therefore it was okay. Thinking I could live like this forever if necessary because that was what was best for the boys.

Then a WhatsApp conversation on a Friday afternoon gets a bit emotional and before I know it, he's coming home because we need to talk. Then he's packing his bags and going to his parents for the weekend. A phone call on Sunday tells me that he is going to live in London. He returns on the Monday and agrees to go to counselling, we went to two sessions but by then it was too late because his mind was made up. I would spend the hour and the £60 crying/begging/losing all self-respect and becoming dangerously dehydrated, he would sit there in stony silence answering questions with questions.

He would still come home each weekend. I would spend the later part of the week incredibly anxious. He would arrive really late on the Friday night, and I would hear him come up the stairs and go straight into the spare room. I would then cry until the next morning when I would way and try and make them as special as possible as if to prove how wonderful his life with us was. We had some lovely weekends with the boys which would raise my hope of reconciliation only to be dashed by him as he left for London on the Sunday night. We had one weekend in particular when he told me everything was going to be alright. We looked at houses on 'Rightmove', talked about booking weekends away just the two of us and he slept in our bed. By the time he came home the next weekend everything had changed again, he couldn't try anymore. I then reached the point where I couldn't do it anymore, I couldn't try for the both of us anymore and I gave him an ultimatum: "Come home and try to rebuild our relationship or make the decision to leave." He made the decision to leave a few weeks before Christmas.

He told me by 'WhatsApp' at 7:30 am on the Thursday Morning. That morning I was due at my friend's house to breakfast mine and her children and take the six of them to school/preschool so she could go to the dentist. I text her to let her know I was on my way but that my husband had finally decided he was leaving me, and I was a bit emotional. She didn't get that message until she got to the dentist. She still feels guilty that she flew out of the door that day, I am grateful because it meant I just had to crack on.

I don't know if you've noticed this about me. But I am not one to bottle up my emotions. I am not one to tackle a problem alone. But to begin with I did. I was so determined to tell as few people as possible because in my mind that made it harder to come back from. I was also embarrassed. Bizarrely my mind flew to people we'd been mates with at university that we hadn't been in contact with for years. "We always said it wouldn't work out. She was way too much of a psycho. Those poor kids. How many have they got? Three? I bet she'd let herself go."

I couldn't help but think I was at fault. I kept apologizing to him although I had nothing to apologies for. I offered to change but had no idea what I should change. I couldn't eat, I couldn't sleep and looking back I don't know how I functioned, but I did. I tried to keep everything ticking over and the boys' lives normal. I couldn't protect them from it all though, there were moments where I couldn't handle it. I had dropped Baby Number One at School and then had to stop and pick something up from Morrison's on the way to take Baby Number Two and Baby Number Three to gymnastics. I never made it to gymnastics. I sat in Morrison's car park and cried. I rang my mum who came to collect the boys and take them to gymnastics and then I carried on crying. I couldn't cope with the stress of it all physically and suffered from terrible migraines. I've been called strong a lot recently but I'm not. I have a strong network of people who hold me up. People have also said, "I couldn't do it!" And if you'd told me a year and a half ago what was going to happen, how I would react and where I'd be now, I wouldn't have believed you. But what else am I supposed to do? I have a house, children, dogs, and a job. I can't just stop!

When I did tell my closest friends they were in shock. He's having a breakdown, a mid-life crisis, just ride it out. But as the weeks went on, they began to change their advice. He needs to show you some respect. You have to decide whether you want to be with someone that can make you feel like this. He can't just walk out on you and the children and not discuss it. But essentially that's what he did.

The Season To...
Be a Broken Mess

I'd like to put the following chapter in perspective. Before the Christmas two weeks after my husband left me, my worst Christmas had been totally my mother's fault. As she reads this, I know what she'll be saying. "It wasn't my fault, it was your grandmothers!" My mum and dad had bought my sister her first car. No one had told me. As we rattled the presents under the tree, I exclaimed in joy. "Imagine if it's car keys!" Next thing, my mum storms out shrieking. "Well done Elisabeth! You've ruined everything!" Apparently, she was actually annoyed at her mother-in-law who had also given the game away but couldn't be cross with her so she took it out on me...Now I know what relationships with mothers-in-law can be like...I understand!

I carried on. That's what mums do, right? They carry on when they feel like death, when snot drips like an open tap down their nose, when they haven't slept properly in days, when their heart is broken and they no longer know if they want to live anymore, they carry on.

I shopped for Christmas presents, I wrapped them, I went Christmas tree shopping with three excitable little boys and then put up and decorated the tree with three even more excitable little boys. I then redecorated the Christmas tree when they were in bed. I cooked, I cleaned, I remembered Christmas parties, Christmas jumper days, and I ran refreshments at the Winter Fair. I went to London for our annual Christmas outing with friends. I bought Christmas cards despite the fact I never send them (I didn't send them), I painfully put-up Christmas cards addressed to my husband and I because of course news hadn't spread yet.

I hosted the in-laws and my (ex) husband for Christmas Eve and Christmas Day. I smiled, I played, I tried to eat and as soon as my three little ones were in bed, I cried.

Christmas Eve is by far the lowest I have ever felt. I didn't want to die but I didn't really want to live either. I had followed our Christmas tradition of giving the boys, my husband and I matching pajamas. We played Monopoly, drank hot chocolate, and listened for the sleigh bells. The boys put their plate out for Father Christmas, said goodnight and I took them up to read their new Christmas stories. By the time I got back downstairs, my in-laws had gone. I tidied up and then I sat in my bedroom with my ex-husband downstairs and phoned my mum. That phone call lasted 37 minutes and I don't think I spoke at all. She says it's the worst thing she has ever experienced; her little girl hysterically crying and not being able to go and get her. I went to bed seriously dehydrated that night.

I did Christmas Day, all of us watching the boys opening their stockings and I can't have been the only person in the room thinking that this will be the last time we do this as a family. I took the boys to church and recharged the batteries before going home. Christmas dinner took seven minutes.

The boys weren't that fussed and as soon as they left the table we were left in stony silence. No one had anything to say. What can you say in that situation? Everyone fought to do the washing up instead. Then once the boys were in bed, I cried again! Then my ex-husband returned to London and life as a single mother who is without her children every other weekend began.

Do I regret hosting Christmas? No. That's the simple answer. One of my brother's was adamant that I should tell my ex-husband and his family to do one. That I should spend Christmas in the safety of my family. I still don't think he gets my decision not too so I'm going to attempt to explain it now. I doubt he'll ever get this far though, there's too much talk about my battered vagina in the early chapters to put him off.

Once I had come to the conclusion that there was nothing, I could do to save my marriage my focus changed. My children were now two, four and five. I do not want them to grow up remembering; arguing, shouting, barbed comments. I never want them feeling torn between the two of us, not wanting to talk about Daddy in front of Mummy and vice versa. I do not want them feeling guilty or thinking that this is their fault in anyway. I know that their parents separating is going to impact them, it can't not. But I want the negative impact to be as small as possible and if I can find a positive impact? I'll blow it way out of proportion. And so…I hosted Christmas for my ex-husband and his parents. The boys had a wonderful day, the grandparents enjoyed it and I survived (just). What was the alternative? For them to have a Christmas without Daddy? Not at home? Not as they'd been talking about since September?

A very wise person (but I'm not sure who so can give them no credit) said of my situation: When your boys are adults they will say to their friends, colleagues, girlfriends, boyfriends, wives and/or husbands that their mum did it all by herself (Barr 36 hours every fourteen days), that they don't know how she did it but that she did an amazing job and that they love her. I think this whenever I'm having a moment, or it all gets too much.

Since then, I have taken the boys to stay with the paternal Grandparents. Again, not something many people do in my position, but I don't regret it. I'm proud of myself. Proud that I can push my feelings to the side and do what is best for my children. If I'm honest I wouldn't have thought myself capable of it.

"You're not coming though are you, Mummy? Because Daddy doesn't like you anymore."

I had no idea how to approach the subject of Daddy and Mummy separating with my boys. They were so little at the time: Two, three and five. After seeking advice (not just from the internet) I made the decision (ex-husband agreed) not to say anything to them and let them ask questions when they were ready.

Life for them hasn't changed. This is not a slight on my ex-husband, but they were used to him not being there. Monday to Friday has always been Mummy. We never shared drop off, pick up, teatime, bath time or bedtime responsibilities. Therefore, the only change to their lives has been Daddy not coming home every weekend but every other, and that when Daddy comes home Mummy leaves.

My ex-husband is not in a position to have the boys anywhere but at our (the boys and mine) home. He arrives late on a Friday night, I leave as the boys wake on the Saturday and then we hand over on a Sunday afternoon. This has been another bone of contention with some family and friends. How can I bare it? Tell him to go and stay in an Airbnb. But again, it's not about me or him. It's about the boys and I think they have adjusted to this routine so well because they do not have to pack bags and go and sleep somewhere new every other weekend. I know that this can only go on for a short time. I'm already relishing in the freedom every other weekend gives me and although I spend a lot of it gallivanting and seeing friends it would be nice to stay at home in peace and quiet. I imagine my ex-husband feels horribly awkward coming back to what is no longer his home and sleeping in the spare bedroom surrounded by every single item that belongs to him. My sister was all for throwing his stuff into the road in bin bags or having a huge bonfire, but I was worried about what the neighbors might say so instead put everything in the spare room. But I must stick to the point. By the time my ex-husband sorts out a second home for the boys they will be very used to Mummy and Daddy not living together anymore, and this will be a steady progression rather than a shock.

The boys and I had out first conversation about it the weekend after Christmas. We were on our way to one of the cousin's baptisms. I had lost the plot that morning my emotions were running high, and I shouted at Baby Number One so loudly that he did a wee. We were in the car on the way and Baby Number One was apologizing. "I'm sorry, Mummy, I'm sorry, I won't do it again." (I'm not even sure

100

what he had done, what I can tell you is that it did not deserve my reaction and yes, I still feel guilty!) I stopped the car and began to explain that I wasn't sad or cross with him. He interrupts me. "Is it because Daddy wants to live in London now?" *How? How are they so clever?*

I didn't think things would even register with the little two but when discussing the upcoming weekend with Baby Number Two I was explaining that it was a 'Daddy Day' and that they were going to a farm park because they had filled up their marble jar (the marble jar now resides with the reward charts, naughty step and time-out timer at the bottom of the 'things that don't work because my children still behave like animals' drawer.) Before I could launch into my 'mummy is going to go and see friends/go to the gym/have a lovely time', he replies, "You're not coming though are you, Mummy? Because Daddy doesn't like you anymore." From the mouth of babies…

Daddy is not a taboo word in our house. As much as it pains me to do, we still talk about happy times with Daddy. Their drawings are still very much of their family as Mummy, Daddy, the three boys and the two dogs and so it should be! Although I've taken down all the photos of my ex-husband and I together there are still some of him and the boys up. My mum has done the same. When I asked her why she said she didn't ever want the boys thinking that her and my dad didn't like their daddy and they couldn't talk about him. She is amazing and I don't know how she does it!

Recently, Baby Number One has been questioning his role in Daddy leaving. He asked me whether Daddy left because he never had his bed to sleep in because he and his brothers were always in it. That broke my heart. I hope I reassured him that it was nothing to do with him. It's hard though, to try and explain something that you don't understand yourself and without portraying their father as a bastard!

I have no idea how they will feel as they get older. I know that I'm going to get the brunt of a lot of it because I'm there. In some ways I hope I do because at least it means they're talking about it. Every time they ask me questions, I spend so much time reflecting and analyzing my answers for fear of saying or doing the wrong thing and damaging them for life. Dramatic I know, but also realistic. I guess, they're stuck with me, and I've done alright so far so we'll muddle through.

Hindsight Is a
Wonderful Thing...

Looking back now I can almost pinpoint the exact moment I think my ex-husbands and my relationship changed. We were on holiday. He was on his phone a lot, working on his laptop whenever we had a quiet moment etc. He was very quiet, we didn't have much conversation and I do remember that feeling of awkwardness that I'd never had with him over the fourteen years we'd been together. I also remember feeling really happy when I walked past him, and he (playfully) pinched my arse because there wasn't much physical contact outside the bedroom. I didn't think much of it at the time. I can hear some of you saying, 'you Muppet' or rolling your eyes but I had three children under the age of five in the sunshine, near open water, forgive me for not having the time to reflect on my husband's behavior.

That unwillingness to chat carried on. We'd obviously have conversations, but I think I probably initiated 99% of them. I knew I was getting desperate when I made up things the boys had done during the day to have a reason to ring him or something to say when he'd get home.

During one our better moments I talked to him about moving closer to London to reduce his commute. This really brought us back together again. Animated conversations, messaging links to right move, looking at train timetables etc. But then I got cold feet. I rely on my family so much. Without them I would have no help with the boys during the week at all. I know I am capable of looking after them by myself but it's much more fun (for them and me) if others are involved. I explained this to my husband. He replied, "Well there's no point in talking about it because it will end in an argument." I was pleased with this response, it meant he'd seen my reasoning behind it. Looking back, he should have fought harder. His reasoning behind moving could have been stronger than mine for staying.

We then have the moments I'm embarrassed to think about:

The constant messaging from a girl/woman/lady from work who he had saved under a man's name in his phone.

How worried I'd be when he went on his lads' weekends away or golf trips. I couldn't say what that particular worry was, cheating, what he'd be saying about me...I don't know.

When he stopped wearing his wedding ring because he had bought a new watch and his hand felt too 'blingy'. I found that wedding ring when sorting out the nursery the other day, laying in the corner with a pile of things ready for the charity shop. I'm so glad that when he took it off, he put it in a safe place to keep.

When I looked at the computer after he'd used it one weekend to find that he'd been researching honeymoon champagne tasting and had entered dates for the summer at the same hotel we'd stayed in to celebrate our engagement and choose our wedding champagne. Apparently, he's going there with his boss. They might look a little odd in a hotel made for couples!

Anyway, like I said, hindsight is a wonderful thing. I realise that I haven't been happy either. Oh, I'm happy day to day. I love being with my boys, I am so grateful that I had the opportunity to be a stay-at-home mum. But I have lost myself slightly. I am an intelligent woman who no longer gets treated like one. I am of average attractiveness but worried about my husband going away with his mates. I am funny and yet have no one to make laugh (that doesn't laugh at Alexa making trump noises. I haven't done anything for myself in six years and yes that's out of choice, but no one has ever asked me if I wanted too. Did I love my husband? Yes, and I still do. Would I ever have chosen for us to separate? No! But as time goes by, I realise that my life isn't going to stop just because he doesn't want to be in it anymore.

Yes, hello Ms Hawes…I'm afraid that I've had to take his playtime on Monday away…

My boys are not angels. They are the type of children you fear bumping into in the tunnel of a dimly lit soft play. They are the type of children that you would only invite for a play date if you could be guaranteed good weather and could therefore keep them in the garden. Baby Number One's teacher recently said that he is focused and hard working in the classroom but as the door opens for play time he turns into a wild animal! They are physical (polite way of saying rough), they always go too far and if I draw a line in the sand then they jump over it whilst farting. Despite all this they are actually really good boys, and I am proud of them. I've always hated parents who bang on about how wonderful their children are. I prefer the ones that call them dick heads and openly have favorites. However, for the purpose of this chapter I need to say that they all appear quite bright, they are polite (most of the time), they can be kind and caring and although a bit rough they are not vindictive at all.

I have been watching their behavior like a hawk. I'm a Primary School Teacher I have seen the impact parents separating can have on children. I know (and hate) that this will have an impact on my children and will do anything I can to minimize that impact. I have analyzed every tantrum, every hit, every inability to share, every rejection of food. Is this happening because their father and I have separated? Then I got a phone call from school: "I'm afraid that I've taken Baby Number One's playtime on Monday away because he upset one of the girls in his class by telling her she was going to die." I hung up that phone and thought *well that's great, we've really managed to fuck him up!* I rang my mum (also a Primary School Teacher) and explained the situation, she laughed...Laughed! She told me to give myself a shake. "He's five!" she said. This is now my mantra.

"I think you should get a solicitor because I have one..."

Being left came as a shock, being asked for a divorce was more of an unpleasant surprise. I mean I knew once he had decided to leave that we would be going down the divorce path I just didn't think it would be quite so soon.

He shouldn't have done this really. Not because it's the type of thing a callous bastard does but because it gave me time. If he'd have said let's sort it out ourselves because we haven't really got anything to fight about, I'd have probably gone along with it. We're thirty-three, we have a house with a fairly large mortgage, two cars, three children and two dogs and fortunately no debts.

I am so glad this didn't happen because my head was fully in the sand. I was so desperate to be amicable that I'd have pretty much given him anything. Obviously, I would have tried to make sure that the boys and I had enough (I had no idea), but I was also really worried about him and making sure he had enough money to buy/rent the two properties he now needed etc.

I've now pulled my head out of the sand and out of my arse. I know what value I have, the importance of all the work I have put into our family and our home over the last seven years and not so long ago I was the bread winner whose salary meant we could get our first mortgage.

I have appointed myself a solicitor and I made the demand that we divorced collaboratively as I felt the result of this would be best for the boys. I am no expert on types of divorce and there are reasons for everyone doing it the way that suits them best. Collaborative divorce means that we both appoint a solicitor trained in the collaborative process and both parties sign up at the start to work on a collaborative process. No court is involved but the outcome is legally binding, and all the meetings have the two parties and their solicitors present. You sit comfortably and problem solve rather than fight each other and this was really important to me especially as he's living in my house every other weekend. As part of the divorce, you each write an anchor statement to read to each other. I'm going to finish my first book with my anchor statement. I wrote this horrifically hungover after the first wedding I'd attended as a single woman. I read it without looking up.

The Boys' Dad

Many people who know me and buy this book because they recognise the name or hear about it on the grapevine may be shocked to find out that my husband and I are separated (probably divorced by the time anyone reads it). I'm not going to lie (why start now) but I've found it really difficult to tell people. I also presumed that people would talk about it. I'll use the work 'gossip' although I like to think people wouldn't do it in a malicious way. Do you remember the days when couples would go 'Facebook Official'? It was a big thing because if you split up then you're break up would be 'Facebook Official' too and shared to all your 'friends'. We announced our engagement, shared pictures of our wedding, birth of our babies, holidays, and date nights on social media but our separation is not something that I have been able to share in this way.

We are no longer 'married' on Facebook but fortunately I found the button which meant *'Lizzie and her husband have ended their marriage'* didn't appear on everyone's News Feed. I know when some couples separate, they delete all images of each other off social media, neither of us have done this. In fact, we're so 'amicable' that he still likes my photos when I do sporadically post them. If you looked at his Instagram, he looks like a happily married man who has a lot of fun with his family. He was.

So, I'm sure the news of us separating will spread. I'm sure people will be shocked, ask questions and have their opinions but I would just rather they did it behind my back. Those that have messaged to find out what happened have all been sent the same response, 'I have no idea, and you'd be better off asking him'. I wonder if they did. Perhaps they can tell me!

This week I had an online meeting with four of the girls I used to play hockey with at university. Two of them were my bridesmaids and are still close friends, they obviously knew. One of them had been told by one of the bridesmaids and she'd been in touch, so I knew she was well informed. I presumed somebody had filled in the final member of our meeting. Turns out they hadn't. About ten minutes in she asks about my husband. Even online it was bloody awkward! I'm sure it will be something I get used too.

What I can't get used to is what do I call him? He's not my husband but I think referring to someone as my ex-husband sounds bitter because you can't help but emphasize the 'ex'. So, I find myself referring to him as 'the boys' dad'. I worry it makes him sound like a sperm donor and not much else, but we'll go with it for now.

Some people have been more difficult to tell than others especially those that you had been pretending everything was alright too. I had some interesting reactions:

- Some were relieved because they thought they'd done something to upset me and now they knew my odd, distant behavior wasn't as a result of them. I felt guilty when they told me this because I hate the thought of upsetting people with my behavior. It's okay now though…They blame him instead.

- My Nana asked my brother if he knew anyone who had a gun. This still makes me laugh, she's quite infirm but I have this image of her as an overweight Bond villain, who carries way too much water in her legs tracking him down.

- Lots of our mutual friends who have known us from the day we got together were disbelieving. I had a lot of messages saying, 'I'm sure it'll work itself out'. It didn't.

- Interestingly, when I told my family I was greeted with radio silence. I thought it is odd at the time until I found out that the moment they had received my message they all immediately phoned my eldest brother to convince him, 'not to do anything'.

I have had an overwhelming about of love and support since the news has spread. Lots of cards, flowers, chocolates, and gin! On Valentine's Day I was inundated (okay just the three). They still keep coming and I am grateful for every single one because honestly? It's shit! Every so often the reality hits me. My husband has left me. I am a single mum to three boys, two dogs and I have absolutely no idea how I'm going to do it alone. Each gift/note/offering of alcohol is a reminder that I am not doing it alone!

My ex-husband/the boys' dad remarked once on how many cards I had been sent. One was from a friend from our university days who he would have considered his friend. I wouldn't say he was annoyed but he was definitely disgruntled by the fact she had sent a card with a supportive message to me. I tried to explain that it's because the desire to separate was so one sided. It made me realise that he doesn't really have a clue what he has done. That he has done this to make himself happy but destroyed my life (and the boys' lives to some extent) to do it. Other people can see it, I wonder when or if he will.

I was worried how my parents would feel about people knowing. My dad is a vicar, my mum a devout Christian. Divorce is not something he believes in. My brothers, sister and I were brought up as part of the Church Family and my God, did we resent everyone having their say on what we did, especially as teenagers. We'd often have comments or unwanted advice on what we wore, if we'd been in trouble at school, our boyfriends or girlfriends etc. I thought that perhaps they would be ashamed to tell people that their daughter's husband had left her. I couldn't be more wrong! They have made a point of telling me time after time how proud they are of me and the boys. They haven't shouted it from the rooftops but by no means have they tried to keep it a secret.

My dad said to me that they had nothing to be embarrassed about. That I had nothing to be embarrassed about. But that he wouldn't like to be my husband or his parents as they explained to people, he had left his wife and three children under the age of six because they'd grown apart and had nothing in common anymore. I can't imagine that's what they will say. There are two sides of every story and I'd love to hear his!

So...Tinder? Bumble? Match?

Thirty-three-year-old mother of three feral boys (one bites), two dogs (neither bite but both smell). Battered vagina. Dislocated coccyx (so that it pokes out at a funny angle) as a result of children having massive heads (see battered vagina). Ski-slope boobs that look like tennis balls in the end of socks. Terrible piles (constant). Map of the Americas in stretch marks across hips and tummy (good for Geography lovers). Varicose veins which are almost invisible unless it's hot/I'm wearing heels/have been on my feet all day (who am I kidding? They're permanent fixtures). Zero confidence (although my friends tell me I'm funny). Zero trust in men. Shit chat (unless it's about my children). Available for 36 hours every other weekend.

I mean...WHAT A FUCKING CATCH!

Obviously, I've thought about my future. Sometimes the thought makes me want to cry, other times I'm more optimistic and can find 'starting again' exciting. My sister is super excited for me, she's convinced that I will find myself and then find someone that worships me. I think she watches too many rom coms. But I'm 33 for Christ's sake and despite the above advert I am reasonably attractive, with clothes on.

I know I don't want to be alone for the rest of my life but more importantly I know I don't want to end up in a relationship where both me and him think he is too good for me.

I know I only want to introduce one other man to my children, and I know I don't want to parent on my own again. I want to share the drop off, pick-ups, clubs, parties, teas, homework, reading, bedtimes etc.

I know that I want to be an amazing mum. I know that I don't want my children to be adversely affected by any of my decisions.

I know that I want to have fun, both with and separate from my boys. I know that I don't want to wallow in grief and be miserable for evermore.

I've looked at those dating sites a few times. Sometimes I even start filling them in, but they ask so many questions, some of which I'm not even sure what the answer is. Do I want more children? I don't bloody know! Am I ready for a new relationship? I don't bloody know! Is marriage important/a necessity? I don't bloody know! The only thing I can say for certain is that I don't want him to smoke!

So, when I feel ready, I will be looking for a relationship, but a relationship for me. Obviously, I'm a mother, I have a body, frown lines and under eye bags to prove it but I'd like someone who sees past all that and to, well...Me. I want to go on dates where I take a handbag not a rucksack full of drinks, snacks, and spare clothes. I want to go to a restaurant I haven't picked because the food arrives really quickly, they have coloring and there's bound to be other children (hopefully noisier ones) in there. I want someone other than my three little boys to think I'm funny and beautiful and want to be with me all the time. But I don't want to need them, just to want them.

Me: "I've read an article saying that after separation it takes 11 weeks for you to start to feel better."
My dad: "Some people never get over it."
Me: "Cheers, Dad!"

Before I sign off you should know that I am actually relishing life as a single mother. After months of not being able to face food (apparently your throat constricting and not being able to swallow is a common consequence of grief) I am now eating and although sometimes the anxiety prevents it, sleeping.

The boys are happy and doing well. I hated the thought of not seeing them every other weekend but now I look forward to it. I have the time to see friends, to travel, to drink and dance, to shower alone and eat and drink nice things without having to share them. They miss me when I'm away and I miss them, and our reunions are always a bit giddy even after 48 hours.

I've been on a date with a man I fancy (and plenty with men I don't) and he's asked to go on another one.

I have the best friends. Friends that have quite literally picked me up off the floor, friends who have let me cry for hours at their kitchen table, friends who have appeared when uninvited because I've been quiet for a few days, friends who have taken my children in a heartbeat because it's all got too much for me. Friends who have opened up their homes to me and my family and renamed their spare bedroom Lizzie's room. Friends who make me laugh, who laugh at me, who never tire of telling me that I am clever, funny, and beautiful even when I don't believe them. Friends who wait for me at every school drop off just to make sure I'm not having a bad day. Friends who join me on weekends away because I can't bear to be near my house even though there's only a single bed where I am going. Friends who undoubtedly have a WhatsApp group where they talk about me, my mental health and how I'm doing. Friends who I know sit at dinner parties and when my situation gets brought up, they have my back and make this very known. Friends who now have my mum and dad's numbers so they can message each other reassuringly. Friends who will buy loads of copies of my book even if they don't need to read it because they've lived it firsthand. Friends who have become family and family that are these friends. Without them there would be no light at the end of this tunnel and because of them that light is becoming closer.

So here it is, the statement I read to my husband on the day we got divorced. I hope that my boys read this book and this statement one day and are proud of me.

I have chosen to work collaboratively because I want to be able to move forward amicably. I would not want to see you put in a difficult situation whether it be financially or regarding the boys. It is very important to me that the boys are put at the forefront of any decision. We are both aware of the impact our separation will have on them, and I want to minimize this impact as much as I can. I hope that in the future we can continue to make parenting decisions together and that we can continue to celebrate milestones together. I hate the idea that our children would ever feel torn between us, and I hope that they never do.

You are an amazing father. The boys' adores and respect you. They love the time you spend together, and I am grateful that you continue to support them in their endeavors (whims). You will be able to give them amazing experiences and I hope as they get older, they continue to have a strong, close relationship with you and your family.

We have been together for fifteen years, the whole of our adult lives. I would like to thank you for all the fun, the laughs, the holidays, for all the times you've comforted me when I've been sad, changed all your plans to come and see me when I've been lonely. You have always had the ability to make me feel safe and see the best in things. I would not be the person I am today if I hadn't had you in my life. What I find saddest about this situation is that I feel as if I am losing my best friend. There is a huge gap in my life without you. There are so many moments each day that I would normally share with you, so many worries I now face on my own and I really do miss you.

I am most grateful for our three beautiful children. The perfect mix of both of us. I love being their mummy and I love that I have been able to stay at home with them. This is entirely down to you and your hard work and for that I cannot thank you enough. My worry is that I won't be able to be there for them like this anymore, I have loved being their teacher, nurse, friend and playmate. I want to be there when they come home from school so I can hear about their days, their successes, their worries. Your hard work has also given us a lovely family home and has given the boys so many opportunities to travel and try new experiences already.

I am happy that you have found a job that gives you a sense of satisfaction but believe me when I say, it is not the only thing you are good at and not your only success story.

I have no idea where we will be in five-or ten-years' time. I hope that you will be happy, I am sad that it won't be with me. I hope our children are thriving, happy and healthy and know that they have two parents who love them very much.

Hold the Phone...
What About the Dogs?

Sorry! I realised I've told you all about the emotional impact this has had on the boys and me without mentioning the other two bitches in my ex-husband's life. Unfortunately, or fortunately he's about as interested in the dogs as he is in me, so they are 100% in my custody. Just the way I like it!

Two and a Half Years Later...

So, two and a half years have now passed since my husband left and I am delighted to tell you all that he soon made the realization that he'd made a huge mistake, we are now living our happily ever after.

Or not! Unfortunately (or fortunately) this is not one of those stories. His career has gone from strength to strength, he is very happy in a new relationship and I am pleased to report that this is not with the young lady messaging him whilst we were on our family holiday. It turns out that she really was just an over-zealous work colleague saved under a nickname! Over time I have become genuinely pleased for him.

My ex-husband and I completed our divorce over Zoom during lockdown. It was brutal. Collaborative or not it was one of the most horrific experiences of my life. Each meeting left me even more broken than the last. I hated having to justify my life choices and unwillingly change the way that I had imagined the future for the boys and myself. But, we did it.

I can now honestly say that my ex-husband and I have a relationship that surpasses any of my expectations. He bought a house locally which he spends every other weekend in with the boys. The boys love him and he continues to be an excellent father. We have reached a point where we can comfortably watch football matches together on the sidelines or sit together for performances. It makes me feel so proud that we can do this for our children although I can understand why other couples can't – it is very hard.

I don't hate him anymore and I don't think I love him anymore either. There is so much of him in the boys (50% would you believe it) not just the way they look but the way they move, their interests and their quirks. I love those three boys so much and with no hesitation would repeat every part of my life which gave me them, including meeting, marrying and divorcing their father.

The boys are happy. I've done a bloody good job. They have their moments but then, who doesn't? They are an absolute credit to me and I will take all that credit.

And me? Well, it has been a rough two and a half years. Once the adrenaline had worn off and I switched from 'survival mode' to 'normal life' about a year after he left, life actually got a bit rougher. Both my physical and mental health took a bit of a hit. It's amazing how your body and mind react to a 'traumatic life experience'. Therapists, my family, and my friends continue to support me as I build myself back up. They are so patient as it really is a case of one foot forward and two steps back. We've all seen a change over the last six months (probably a result of the drugs) and I am beginning to feel more confident and happy with the person that I am. I was going to say I felt more like my old self but I'm so different to her now that that just wouldn't be the case.

And there we have it, I really will leave you now (I know I said that about 500 words ago). I also have a new man in my life. I am trying not to let my past affect my future but that is easier said than done. Fortunately I have managed to find myself a non-judgemental, patient, and kind chap. Between him, my boys and the wonderful people who surround me I feel hopeful for the future. That is not something I expected to feel two-and-a-half-years later.